VIOLENCE IN HISTORY, CULTURE, AND THE PSYCHE

Spring Journal Books
Analytical Psychology &
Contemporary Culture Series

Series Editor:
Thomas Singer, M.D.

VIOLENCE
IN HISTORY, CULTURE, AND THE PSYCHE

Essays

Luigi Zoja

Translated by

John Peck and Victor-Pierre Stirnimann

with an Afterword by

John Peck

Spring Journal Books
New Orleans, Louisiana

Published by
Spring Journal, Inc.
627 Ursulines Street #7
New Orleans, Louisiana 70116
Tel.: (504) 524-5117
Website: www.springjournalandbooks.com

Cover design by:
Michael Mendis
24 Blackfriars Street
London, Ont. N6H 1K6, Canada
e-mail: mmendis@rogers.com

Cover art:
The Riders of the Apocalypse (oil on canvas) by Vasko Taskovski
Image © 2008, The Bridgeman Art Library International, Ltd.

Back cover:
Photograph of Luigi Zoja, © Basso Cannarsa

Printed in Canada
Text printed on acid-free paper

Library of Congress Cataloging-in-Publication Data Pending

To

JAMES HILLMAN

A NOTE ON THE TRANSLATORS

Chapter 2, "Trauma and Abuse: The Development of a Cultural Complex in the History of Latin America," was translated from the original Italian by Victor-Pierre Stirnimann for an earlier publication. The rest of the chapters and the Introduction have been translated specifically for this volume by John Peck.

Contents

Acknowledgments

I would like to thank Thomas Singer, the series editor, for selecting this book to be the inaugural volume in Spring Journal Books' new series, Analytical Psychology and Contemporary Culture. Spring Journal Books publisher Nancy Cater has been unfailing in her encouragement in seeing the book into print. John Peck and I also wish to extend particular thanks to Sylvia Ruud and Michael Mendis for their expert editing, and to Michael as well for all the other work he has done in putting this volume together. Finally, I want to express heartfelt gratitude to John Peck, my translator, without whose intuitive and comprehensive understanding of my ideas this English edition would not be possible. Thanks are also due to Victor-Pierre Stirnimann for permission to reprint his translation of the paper that appears as Chapter 2 in this publication.

The papers in this collection were originally presented at various conferences and other venues between 2000 and 2008.

In abbreviated form, Chapter 1, "Violent Hearts: The Divided Soul of America," was delivered as the keynote lecture at the conference "Violent Hearts: The Divided Soul of America," sponsored jointly by The Honors College at the University of Houston and The Jung Center, September 30-October 1, 2005. A version of the paper was published subsequently in *Spring 78—Politics & the American Soul* (Fall 2007): 51-68.

The contents of Chapter 2, "Trauma and Abuse: The Development of a Cultural Complex in the History of Latin America," was first delivered as the keynote address at the 2nd Latin American Congress of Analytical Psychology in Rio de Janeiro, June 2000. It was first published as "Trauma and Abuse: A Psychological Approach to a Chapter of Latin American History" in the *Journal of Jungian Theory and Practice* 3, no. 1 (2001): 39-49. It was subsequently modified to incorporate the theme of "cultural complexes" for inclusion in *The Cultural Complex: Contemporary Jungian Perspectives on Psyche and*

Society, ed. T. Singer and S. L. Kimbles (New York: Brunner-Routledge, 2004), pp. 78-89. This modified version is reprinted here by permission of the publisher and the editors.

An abbreviated version of Chapter 3, "The Duel and Honor," was delivered as a talk at the University of Brno in the Czech Republic in 2003.

An earlier version of Chapter 4, "Nightmares," was delivered as a presentation at the international conference, "ELEMENTI—Acqua Aria Terra Fuoco," sponsored by the Municipality of Parma's Department of Mobility and Environment and the Ministry for the Environment and Territorial Conservation, in Parma, May 17-21, 2006.

An earlier version of Chapter 5, "Reductivism: Against Ismene," was delivered under the title "Reductionism: A Western Disease?" at the Eranos Conference 2006 in Ascona, Switzerland, June 18, 2006.

Chapter 6, "The Clash of Civilizations? A Struggle between Identity and Functionalism," was originally presented as a paper at the conference "È Scontro di Civiltà?" organized by Il Sole and the Italian Center for Analytical Psychology in Milan, October 23, 2007.

Chapter 7, "Almachius and the Demon: Mass Entertainment and Violence-as-Spectacle," was originally delivered as a paper at the Eranos Conference 2008, "Perspectives on Violence and Agression," at Ascona-Moscia, Switzerland, June 15, 2008.

—Luigi Zoja
August, 2009

A Note from the Series Editor

Thomas Singer, M.D.

In our rapidly changing contemporary world, analytical psychology is confronted ever anew with the challenge of remaining relevant. To take on this challenge, Spring Journal Books has created the Analytical Psychology & Contemporary Culture Series. The goal of the series is to bring analytical psychology into a cross-fertilizing dialogue with the fundamental issues of our time. The series will explore the multiple, interpenetrating relationships between history, mythology, politics, economics, sociology, and the arts as they express themselves in contemporary culture. At the heart of our mission is the creative exploration of the psyche's response to a world in rapid transition from the evolving perspectives of analytical psychology.

Luigi Zoja's *Violence in History, Culture, and the Psyche* is the perfect inaugural volume for the new series. This collection of Zoja's lectures probes in depth one of the core issues that vex contemporary life: violence in all its myriad forms. Zoja has circumambulated the globe in his travels and in his quest to apply the techniques and insights of analytical psychology to understanding the conflicts and aspirations of the early 21st century in a broad historical, mythological, and psychological context, and he thus brings a breadth of vision to bear on this terrifying subject.

Negritude is not biological in its essence. … It is a way of living history within history. … Chromosomes hardly count. But I believe in archetypes, in the worth of everything buried in the collective memory of our peoples and in the collective unconscious. I do not believe that one enters the world with a blank brain in the same way that one arrives with empty hands, but that one is shaped by the power of cumulative historical experience and the lived experience transmitted by culture.

—Aimé Césaire†

---

†From a speech presented at the *Première conference hémisphérique des peuples noirs de la diaspora*, Florida International University, Miami, February 26, 1987.

Introduction

Great events, even if named for odd sorts of things, channel eternal images into the furrow of history. The myths that proclaim them anew reveal the oldest tendencies of humankind. These are conditioned by birth, physically and psychologically: we call the bodily ones instincts, and the corresponding mental ones archetypes.

Nothing is more terrible, fascinating, and overwhelming than the human need to attack, to hate, and especially to kill. Violence is a boundary archetype, the expression of a force that is *life and death* at the same time. Tendencies toward wisdom, love, irony, and solidarity embody "only" the aspects of life, whereas that very same life depends upon the destructive impulse.

In that sense, the inquiry into violence is the most important kind of psychological research. I shall not lapse into the kind of sophistry that would turn this inquiry into some kind of program for bringing to an end the repeated massacres that have punctuated human history. On the contrary, an honest psychological understanding compels us to conclude that violence is innate in human nature; throughout history, it has manifested itself in every kind of social group that humans have formed. One of the principal tasks of any society, then, is to set definite limits for it.

On the one hand, acknowledging the inevitability of violence can be dangerous, because it can lead to despair and resignation, thereby giving free rein to violence. To imagine that violence can be done away with, on the other hand, is a supremely risky over-simplification. The greatest atrocities of the past have been predicated upon the denial of violence as natural or inherent in humanity. Springing from the arrogance that has led Western civilization to believe it can shape nature and history, utopias and ideologies have repeatedly set about creating *the new man*: a robotic creature stripped of evil, an unconscious throwback to the mythical primal man who existed in Eden before the Fall.

Utopian dreams, however, pose a paradoxical inconvenience: there are some who will not be assimilated easily or allow themselves to be turned into robots. These require a dose of intensified violence to accelerate the disagreeable transition. Unlike God, when man "creates," he is always in a hurry, or at any rate in an altered state of mind. In Europe's religious wars, in the Anglo-Saxon colonization of North America or the Spanish effort to the south, in the fascist version of nationalism, in the thrust of communist regimes into Eastern Europe and Asia, the violent elimination of adversaries was not the exception but the rule. We cannot dismiss this monumental omnipresence of violence by saying that it was the result of some mistake, or that it was not included in the original teachings of Christ or even, generally speaking, in those of Marx. We are faced with something inherent, something structural.

Intellectual discussions frequently revolve around whether the great atrocities of history were driven by faiths clothed in ideologies or vice versa. That, however, is not the point. The center of gravity for reflection on these matters should shift to the fact that those who have believed strongly in their principles, and have been bent on applying them, have also frequently believed that one can mold a new kind of creature, one that is substantially more rational but also more peaceful, constitutionally fond of solidarity and kindly disposed to neighbors: a non-violent genetic mutation. Unconsciously, however, this has also been a mutation of the omnipotent tendency of human will—in fact, of divine will—by virtue of wanting to re-enact the creation story in the Book of Genesis. And such a pursuit of omnipotence, however many praiseworthy half-measures it may attend to, is difficult to carry out, because it loses its way in morbid selfsatisfaction and self-adoration. This tendency constitutes the unavoidable dark side of the shining personality. We call that side the unconscious shadow, but its effects are devastatingly real. Few perversions have drenched the streets of Europe with as much blood as has this shortcut to paradise. So, an awareness of the extent to which violence is endemic in all of us is an important aid in avoiding the naïveté that, paradoxically, ends up producing atrocities.

Even this very general treatment of both our destructive impulses and the archetypal perspective—which tends to seize on their commonality through time—cannot, however, ignore the enormous leap that violence has taken in the wake of modernization. In the first place, technology has served to multiply violence by placing in human hands missiles that can take millions of lives in a matter of seconds while bypassing our inhibitors of last resort: in launching such a missile, one goes into action from an armchair in front of a computer screen, seeing no splatters of blood or blown-off limbs, hearing no cries of agony. Secondly, violence grows on its own, from its own momentum, rather than from ideology or secularism. The plunge onwards into the more massive forms of violence is not exclusively technological, but also anthropological. Paradoxically, the "century of light," or the Enlightenment, leads to the violence of the "century of night," or the Endarkment, a name that perhaps should be assigned to the century of massacres only recently ended.[1]

As for whether ideology can be seen as a secular religion (and vice versa), the religious perspective frames matters in terms of divine will while the ideological one speaks of human will, a difference that carries considerable weight. For example, there is debate over whether the Spanish conquest of Mexico—which in a few generations reduced the original population of the country by nearly 95%[2]—ought to be regarded as genocide. This devastation resulted from a convergence of events, at once military, socio-economic (the eradication of traditional practices of sustenance and the onset of forced labor), psychological (described in Chapter 2 of this book), and to a great extent sanitary (epidemics of illnesses imported from Europe, against which the local inhabitants had no barriers of immunity). To be sure, the decimations accomplished by smallpox and similar infections were not part of the Spanish agenda, but they were nevertheless greeted mainly with delight by the Spanish authorities (and viewed as an act of God on behalf of the conquerors).

In other epochs, the great plagues were viewed as expressions of God's will. Not only was this attribution made by virtue of the failure to grasp the mechanisms of infection, but in circular fashion, the archetypal tendency to think of each successive outbreak as an expression of divine will stifled, in its turn, the scientific attitude that was necessary to handle deadly bacteria in a controlled manner. Only in relatively recent times—and fortunately to a limited extent—have humans plotted chemical and biological warfare. The fact that its application has been limited is due not so much to its inhumanity as to the difficulty of controlling its effects and the possibility that those who use such methods may themselves be exterminated on the rebound. Were it not for this purely *technical* barrier, with the *theological* obstacle by now removed, human beings would have supplanted God as the unleashers of deadly epidemics, and the 20th century would have been even darker than it was—and already it is the darkest ever known.

Genocide is an extreme form of violence, which seeks to get rid of not a specific individual or a particular group of individuals, but an entire population as such. Its definition as a specific criminal act is relatively recent: it dates back only to 1948, when the United Nations adopted the Convention on the Prevention and Punishment of the Crime of Genocide, which was pushed to completion by the efforts of Raphael Lemkin. Few debates in human history have compelled both conscience and consciousness, driven by a new concept, to take sides in a confrontation with extreme forms of evil.

One cannot, however, fail to notice how polarization around the idea of genocide can stir up historical, judicial, and ethical debate at the risk of diverting attention from the enormity of the very crime in itself. Insofar as it arises from a recent decision among international political powers—and from judicial definition—this debate on genocide can become abstract, almost philological. Central texts like those by Todorov, Stannard, Power, and Kiernan,[3] while they are persuaded of the ultimate tragedy of human nature and the responsibility that it places upon us, do not lead us all the way down to bedrock. They only provoke polemical responses by framing the discussion in terms of the agenda they have in common, namely, to apply the label "genocide" to certain historical events. When this kind of dispersal begins to confine the problem to side issues, I believe it is useful to return to the fountainhead and its absolute dimension, that of violence.

Is it necessary to debate whether the extermination of Native Americans during the colonial period, of Armenians in the Ottoman Empire, or of kulaks under Stalin—like the extermination of the Jews—constitutes genocide, when the monstrous number of victims and the identity of the perpetrators have been definitively established? Apart from the framing of these crimes within judicial proceedings, the central point is that their essential monstrosity should not be denied. It is not the perfidy, ideology, or complicity of certain groups that succeeds in erasing historical crimes. It is simply the normal human mind, which has a threshold for the toleration of horror, beyond which it switches off and slips into negation.

Nothing demonstrates this better than language—and with it the collective unconscious articulated through language by an entire people. Among the major European languages, the words that refer precisely to extreme forms of violence are *neutral* or objective in their derivation, maintaining a safe distance from horror. *La strage,* Italian for "slaughter," branches out from the same etymological stem that produced *la strada* (street or road). It indicates the act of paving—covering an area with slabs, or carpeting a floor—and the "paving stones" may just as well be corpses. The corresponding word in German is *das Gemetzel,* bloodbath, and the verb *metzen* (from which comes *Metzger,* butcher) is simply the act of slaughtering an animal. The same process of word formation in English produces *carnage* (which likewise indicates an animal cut up for meat), and in French *le massacre,* which stems either from the same root as *la mazza,* the Italian word for the maul or bludgeon, the traditional tool for butchering animals, or from the Arabic *maslakh,* a shambles or slaughterhouse. Instinctively, the human being who kills his or her own kind wants above all to put the event aside, immediately desiring to forget it all, turning away to sleep it off quietly. Hence, whenever possible, we avoid using words that go on feeding the emotions. Killing becomes a material, technical, statistical fact: the cold registers of Auschwitz are simply the most chilling form of this universal tendency to denial.

In confronting the problem of violence, one must do battle with haste—that ally of forgetting—and rediscover the natural passage of time. As the final chapter of this book suggests, in the absence of cultural antibodies violence can spread like a plague epidemic, breaking out at dreadfully frequent intervals. Slow and laborious, instead, is the exit that we must make from the collective intoxications that spill forth from violence. And so, then, deliberate and toilsome, and for the most part individual, are those contributions we are called on to make to the work of prevention.

CHAPTER ONE

Violent Hearts: America's Divided Soul

DIVISION

Why is Odysseus called unique, timeless, and modern in every age? Not, according to the commonplace, because he is intelligent. Are modern people always bright and the ancients dim-witted? Not because he is a hero; every age enumerates this theme to the point of tedium. And not even because he is, in contemporary terms, an ordinary man, an antihero. Thersites, a common man, antiheroic in knowing the shadow of destiny but also the light of common sense, is already present in the first episodes of the premier poem of the West. In fact, it will be Odysseus himself, in the second book of the *Iliad* (ll. 212-277), who castigates this figure for daring to stir up the battle-weary Greek army against the king's authority.

The answer to our question turns out to hinge upon our theme. That is, Odysseus is ageless because of internal division or splitting. He is hardly compromised by that fact; indeed, he thrives on it.

Odysseus is at home in every era because, in his complexity, many personalities belong to him. Each character in Homer is allotted a fixed set of adjectives that elaborate a single quality, and that are meant to help the oral performer of the poem by supplying rhythmic promptings and supporting his imagination during oral performance. But Odysseus is an exception. No single focus exists for his characterization, such as physical prowess. Instead, a whole array of qualities is present, forming a complex whose parts intermingle: *poly-tlas* (he can bear many things), *poly-tropos, poly-metis, poly-mechanos* (he can cleverly invent or create many things, he can think his way through anything, he can travel anywhere)—which is to say, he has many identities.

He is fierce and destructive, like the ancient heroes; in fact, we know that his name means "that which hates" (*Odyssey* 19.406-409). In the end, however, once he has conquered, he shows a surprising respect for the dead (22.411ff.) and for survivors (22.371 ff.). This sensitivity toward external enemies is a mirror reflection of his respect for internal adversaries. Odysseus battles opponents but also fights with himself, in that way opening a door onto a psychic dimension. While the masterworks of many national literatures ignore the soul's complexity, and the Hebrew and Christian scriptures enlist the soul in the service of the divine, the first great Greek author, who as a man of the 8th century B.C.E. did not know the written medium, already tried to describe what today we would call a psychological process. Perhaps from his attempts came the Greek idea of *psyche*.

Naturally, Homer did not carry out a psychological analysis as we understand it today. Had he employed modern psychological terms, imaginatively impoverished as they are, his narrative poems would most likely have been entirely forgotten. He makes direct use of symbols, which say far more than do the abstractions that explain them. In that sense, the novelty of Odysseus is situated in the very language of human contradictions—the "I" that would but cannot, the compromises among internal pressures—2,600 years before psychoanalysis.

The author whom we call Homer must have been an extraordinary poet and psychologist. He devoted fully half of his work to describing a single character—Odysseus—most likely attributing to him qualities that must have been his own: introspection and the ability to identify with others. He made the first attempt to tell the story, not of a war, a myth, or a god, but—to use the first word of the *Odyssey*—a man: *ándra*. And the man he described was not a unified being.

Confronted with mortal danger, not every Homeric hero goes on the attack as do the figures in modern action films. Some of them, given to reflection, hang back. In the decisive duel of the *Iliad* (22.96-366), Hector fails to confront Achilles. Consulting his own heart, he asks himself if he might make peace with his enemy. Imagining that this would mean loss of honor, he tries to change his mind. But giving in to fear once again, he turns back to beleaguered Troy, finally rebuking his heart and forcing himself to wait for Achilles. Odysseus, however, behaves this way not only in the face of death but rather consistently. In contrast to the ancient heroes, who immediately look for some way to impose themselves on an adversary, Odysseus knows how to listen for the voice of the other man—the other within you, the other you have before you—to make his acquaintance. And, based on that new knowledge, he knows how to gain new opportunity.

To accept the soul's inherent division, to elaborate on it and turn it into a rich resource, is the new super-weapon. Odysseus is both one figure and many figures (*poly-*) in one.

The fact that Odysseus disguises himself and presents himself under names that are not his own is therefore not simply a narrative expediency. Odysseus in fact invents the "capacity to put on another man's clothes," sometimes to elicit his sympathy, at other times to psych him out and beat him at the first opportunity. This capability is a prerequisite, whether for the organization of a non-tyrannical society—like that of the Greeks—or for winning calculated victories over an enemy. This very characteristic has awarded the advantage to the West over millennia.[1]

If a shadow happens to fall across the street, the dog either barks or does not bark. Likewise, if a scare befalls a man, he either cries "Help!" or does not. But the man who has cried for help will go on asking himself, with one part of his mind, if that was the right thing to do. Only the stupid or the fanatical fail to realize that the inner voices that contradict each other are a great gift from the psyche.

The fact that 20th-century psychiatry has given rise to both psychoanalysis—which constantly reveals the existence in us of a counter-position, the unconscious—and the diagnostic system of classification is one of the paradoxes of modernity. These classifications would have us believe that everything is simpler: that the person is the category rather than, as psychoanalysis would say, the person is the category but also, in his or her unconscious, something else.

One of the most debatable psychiatric classifications is precisely the one that takes up pathological ambivalence. Naturally, any psychic condition has its exaggerated expression, and the exaggeration of ambivalence is paralysis. But ambivalence is not only an ordinary human condition; it can also express the highest degree of creative capacity. I have written elsewhere seeking to show how the greatest harm coming from mass entertainment is due precisely to its loss of the ambivalence, the insolubility of the most important human dilemmas, that was the strength of tragedy.[2] Mass entertainment replaces this strength with the predictable Hollywood hero.

Our major works of art tell us in various ways about our absurd ordinariness: only the gods are absolutely beautiful or entirely good. The superiority of human beings to the ingenuous gods of antiquity rests, in a certain indefinable way, with a single attribute: being torn between opposite modes of being. Something of the same kind of superiority is true of artistic representation—its indefiniteness—next to the common kind, which is definite. Leonardo's *Mona Lisa* is a masterpiece in part because it expresses happiness and sadness at the same time, indistinguishably. So are Euripides' *Medea*, for being simultaneously heroic and perverse, and Goethe's *Faust*, for describing an ambivalent soul, a force that wills evil but works goodness. Truly great creations are embodiments of the intricate profundity of the human being.

Therefore, let us draw the following inference. The world of the machine "wants" to supplant the human world. Being operational seems more important than being. For the operation of a machine, whether it is with the lever for forward or for reverse, there is only one way. We are surrounded by devices that condition us to think that this is the only possibility. But the human soul is exactly the combination of both levers, of the two functions—going back and going forth—engaged at the same time. This makes it a little slower and more cumbersome than a machine, but infinitely more interesting.

Homer's figures are among the best known of all, even if no religion or powerful nation has adopted them. They are known because they are human; in their simple mental processes we can still recognize ourselves. We take part in their dramas not only because of their staying power, but also, as Bruno Snell has said, because of *recognition*.[3] In line with Snell's idea, Jacqueline de Romilly has observed that Odysseus's admonition "Be patient, my heart!" initiated what today we call psychology.[4]

Odysseus has returned to Ithaka, among the parasitical suitors who deplete its wealth and lie in wait for his wife. Furious to the core, he would like to grab the sword and avenge himself immediately: he is a *violent heart*, as our chapter title puts it. But he knows that this would be suicidal. His heart yelps like a mother hound defending her young. Like the dog's master, Odysseus forces it to be quiet. He does not stop at simply chiding it. He knows that it is right, but that its rightness is only one among many good reasons for acting. Motive determines the objective; prudence decides on the timing. He orders his heart to sustain him (*Odyssey* 20.18). Odysseus differs from conventional heroes in that he listens, and also waits. Homer describes his thinking as being like a ball that volleys back and forth continually "between head and heart" (*kata phrena kai kata thymon*).

In the Western tradition, division within the soul has been literally demonized; European languages define evil with terms derived from the Latin *diabolus* (devil), in its turn derived from the Greek *dia-ballo*, that which divides things. However, a conscious psychic division, accepted by the ego, is also our richness and humanity. It is the fertile field in which our ambivalence grows, our complexity and, finally, our creativity. *Di-vision*—separation into two parts—is the necessary ground for *dis-course*—the word that runs or flows between two parties. The prefix here, *dis-*, is Latin for separation. Only that ground which has been divided by the plowshare can receive any seed.

Vertical division, those passages from deeper levels of the soul to ones less profound, may also correspond to *horizontal* divisions, over time.

In this respect, too, Odysseus is the forerunner of Western vitality. His life is made up of radical shifts in activity and changes of place. After growing up on Ithaka, he endures ten years of war at Troy. Ten years of return voyaging come after that. Finally, his reign on Ithaka is to be followed, according to prophecy (*Odyssey* 23.264-284), by another long voyage and another return. His life with Penelope is interrupted by a long bachelor phase, during which he spends one year with Circe and seven with Kalypso before returning to Penelope. He goes from being king to being a wanderer and beggar, then king once more and again wanderer, at long last making a definitive homecoming.

A prefiguration of Western man? Better yet, a prefiguration of the West's own West, the United States of America, where the courage and insatiable curiosity of Odysseus became the national soul: a way of being with no geographical or historical precedents. Inheriting the command to "Go West!" the new man has stayed on the move. With arrival at the Pacific Ocean, the *West* came to an end, but the *Go!* went on living, becoming a commandment, a mission. Not a journey, but America's stable essence—so much so that a foreign visitor on an American highway is very likely to hear the police say, "Keep moving!"[5]

The typical American citizen changes his place of residence more often than the citizens of any other country in the world, changes marital status, religion, and profession more often as well, in every era and in all regions of the country. He or she changes these things—sometimes even sexual orientation—because of a belief in improvement or betterment, faith in a future greater than the past, a faith inconceivable to a Greek or an Italian but obligatory to the Pilgrim Fathers and their descendants.[6]

To accomplish this mission, however, one must divide up time: one must close the door to the past and vault the fence of the future. The search for purification from evil has driven Americans to eliminate the internal "other." But this liquidated factor returns as the "other" in time. The search mission abandons England as impure in order to build a pure society, but it also leaves a filthy past for a polluted future. *Time* divides itself into separate *times*. In the United States, life can be diced up into very different periods, such that one cannot come to grips with them. The extraordinary lability of spaces and times, into which the American soul adventures at the behest of its original commandment, is a possibility without equal, but also—something less talked about—an anxiety without definition. To pull up stakes, leave it all behind for the new thing, and with it every time to secure rebirth also becomes an act of violence, a death for the former life. It is an endless revolution. And revolutions are always violent; the old king, the outworn condition, must die. The anxiety of separation or division is therefore the absolute American anguish: an inner panic about losing identity, about taking on too much change, a fear of falling into the void that rises from having lived in too many spaces, of discovering that a country that has crumbled on every side no longer occupies any place.

At the origins of Western history, the Greeks were divided into independent city-states. They frequently made war with each other, but little happened in these wars. The conquering city did not incorporate the defeated one, and the dimensions of cities did not grow very much. Having invented democracy, the Greeks passed the better part of their time in the civic square discussing the nature of life in society, with each citizen advancing his own opinion. They knew all too well that society, if it grew too large, risked becoming ungovernable and ceding power to a tyrant.

Every four years, the Greeks gathered themselves at Olympia; like champion duelists from armies, they gave themselves over to literary and athletic contest. Unity and division were two faces of Greek identity.

Once Greek society had grown in scale, democracy was abandoned for mon-archy (*monos* meaning not just one but *only* one). Much the same thing happened to the Roman republic. Western history had to wait until the American and French revolutions to see dualisms, and differences in general, fully recognized again. History, however, has brought the two continents to deal with the problem of division in different ways. Europe was always divided into nations that were strong rivals. Infant French democracy immediately resisted internal squabbles, suppressing them with terrorism or projecting them outside, thus contributing to a paranoid nationalism. Wars among the nation-states continued through the first half of the 20th century. At that point Europe, without any illusions, plunged itself into a massacre bloodier than all the rest in human history. Thereafter, it began to construct a federation that was post-national, post-ideological, post-religious, and post-heroic.

The United States, by contrast, did not experience genuine external threats; consequently the first phase of its history did not lend itself to aggressive nationalism. The single mortal risk was internal division. The struggle against division has remained an absolute priority, continuing uninterrupted until today.

Such a fundamental American word as "divisive" is not translatable into the European languages; it is simply not to be found in the dictionaries. Another difficulty encountered by Europeans who explore the American language is the discovery that the substantive plural of the country's name is followed by verbs in the singular number: *is*, and not *are*. History has more logic than pure grammar does; it was after the Civil War that the singular number became the correct form.

The USA and Europe have therefore marched off in opposite directions. While from the beginning the United States was less aggressive and more tolerant than Europe, in a certain sense their positions today have changed places. The turning points are the Civil War in the United States and the two World Wars in Europe.

Today, concepts such as *federal* and *federation* (from Latin *foedus*, oath) arouse different emotions in the European and the American unconscious. For Europe it connotes a secular concept, contractual in the manner of a civil marriage. It is a freely chosen union, which in the same free manner can be dissolved again. (See Article 60.1 in the projected EU Constitution.) The American concept of federation, in contrast, remains quasi-religious, absolute, like Catholic marriage. The preamble to the Articles of Confederation for November 15, 1777 speaks of *perpetual union*. The preamble to the Constitution, September 17, 1787, speaks of *a more perfect union*. For the post-religious European, qualities such as *perpetual* and *perfect* are not human but divine. From that viewpoint, therefore, the American Constitution contains no provisions that allow for exit from the Union, because it is a religious document—and, like Catholic marriage, is religiously integralist.

Psychodynamics, let us remember, function by reproducing oppositions. If consciousness accepts only one aspect of a polarity, the other aspect sets up a clamor in the unconscious, until repression no longer works and there is some kind of explosion. Issuing from the death of Greek democracy, the equilibrium between unity and division has suffered throughout the West, first in Europe and now even more so in America.

America was born out of two originating traumas: the religious separation first from Rome and then from London, and the separation of the thirteen colonies from the English monarchy—and then from two historical fractures: the Civil War, and an ethnic mix composed of three hostile races. Because of these facts, America in its own collective unconscious has chiseled into stone the motto, *Never again division!*

Over time, this culture of unity at all costs has transformed itself into a one-sided negation of shadow, that is to say, of divisiveness or divisions, which are an ordinary human reality. Being further along into a future from which no one can escape, America is experimenting for the first time with new kinds of division. It has encountered the war between the sexes, which had not existed before; new rivalries among ethnic groups and differentials between social classes, which are growing with explosive speed;[7] and a divide between free persons and persons in prison that has no historical precedent[8]—indeed, the number in American jails is proportionally eight times the number jailed in Europe. Analytical psychology has this to say about the situation: whoever refuses to accept the presence of opposites is destined to encounter them in pathological forms.

Perhaps it is no accident that the most typical new syndrome to come along in America is that of Multiple Personality Disorder (*DSM IV* 300.14). America prohibits the psyche from dividing within itself. Since many people are not going to be following orders, at some point they will definitely be calling in sick.

Even in war, the real winner is probably the unconscious, which manifests a crude, sarcastic irony. The major preoccupation of politicians is that a war, which bit by bit kills people, is going to be *divisive.* Yet as time goes on, a war not only brings about death and division, it piles up literally divided corpses, blown to bits. In modern warfare, fewer and fewer victims are killed by conventional weapons, and always more by bombs. It is said that tools and other implements are extensions of the human body. Similarly, more advanced implements are extensions of more primitive ones. This is particularly true of weapons: if the sword is an extension of the arm, the rifle is an extension of the sword. But a bomb strikes indiscriminately at a distance, because it has lost even this shred of meaning: it is simply the extension of hatred.

To the dead blown into a hundred pieces it is simply impossible to offer even the proper rites of burial. The dignity of such ritual, even in Homer's day, was still more sacred and inviolable than the respect for life itself. Having made it a priority to multiply our terrifying violence by technological means, we are stripping ourselves of those burial customs which not even the Neanderthals did without.

From *E pluribus unum* to *Ex uno plurimi*: The Generation of Opposites

If Odysseus is the character who best prefigures the American spirit, the epic poem that most influenced the founding fathers was not the *Odyssey* but the *Aeneid.*[9] In contrast to Odysseus, who generated a myth, the figure of Aeneas—who is probably mythic in his own right—already came equipped with an historical and ideological mission. The success of Aeneas's mission put down the roots of a tree that has grown through the millennia. The twin criteria of mission and success story have been an excellent match for the intentions of the founding fathers, and correspond to the development of the American spirit throughout the nation's history.

The *Aeneid* is the first example of a convincing and coherent construction of national history. It expresses the history and ideology of the program of Octavian Augustus, the founder of the Roman Empire and the most enlightened of its emperors, who promoted literature. As often noted, it also offers an epic model for the birth of the American nation. Surviving the Greeks who would have exterminated them and trusting in the gods who protected them, the Trojans of Aeneas embark on an adventurous westward voyage, with no other compass than faith in the divine mission entrusted to them. They arrive on the coast of Italy, the land promised to them by the gods. When they encounter native peoples, they conquer them by force of arms, but end up making compromises and alliances. The love of the founding fathers for the *Aeneid* was such that they inscribed, on the Great Seal as well as on the dollar bill, three phrases in Latin instead of English, two of which they freely drew from Virgil.[10]

As we know, if the political history of the United States begins in 1776, its cultural history begins much earlier, with the arrival of various radical Protestant groups on the coast of New England.

Ships from the countries of Latin Europe carried only men to the New World's shores. These men killed off the native males and forced the women to become slaves and concubines, as well as the mothers of their bastard sons, only sometimes making them their legitimate wives. Giving birth to a legitimate society into which illegitimate children were born was the order of the day. This foundational contradiction has relegated Latin America to inferiority in the view of the Northern Hemisphere, to a greater extent than either military or economic domination. This stain has made the presence of sin and darkness—already accepted, with resignation, out of Catholic tradition—as routine and inevitable as the changing of the seasons.

How different were the Anglo-Saxon immigrants to the New World! They were fleeing the corruption of the Roman Church and the British monarchy, and were dedicated to re-establishing both society and religion. They arrived as families and chose to keep sexuality in the channels laid down by God. The colonists' founding spirit and westward conquest, their subjugation of native peoples on new territory for a divinely ordained mission, echoed the Trojan-Augustan program but at the same time inaugurated a grandiose political experiment: a system of government made up of free and equal individuals who did not accept the dictates of external tyrants. But they were also trying out a grandiose *psychological experiment*, a system of government for the soul, which eliminated the corresponding internal tyrant, evil itself, which they left behind with the rulers of Europe.

The foundational project of the United States was not only political, as it was for most other countries, but also missionary and puritanical. It was the project which today is called *civil religion* and its continuation. From the viewpoint of analytical psychology, the project of a radical elimination of evil—that is, the definitive separation and negation of the so-called shadow—is inevitably dangerous. Omnipotence sooner or later runs into impotence. It feels constrained to take measures that become ever more radical, and more violent, and in the end to introduce, under the forms of violence, precisely the evil that it wanted to do away with.

In a simple society, one is better able to cultivate the need for purity. This the colonists understood very well, and so, in contrast to the Spaniards, they sought to keep themselves distinct from the natives, driven by motives that were moral rather than political. The original geographic and demographic circumstances of the USA differed from those of all other conquering peoples known to history. Over time, the Americans were able to incorporate new territories into the Union without any apparent compromises, placing the native peoples on reservations. The political enterprise and the psychological project went hand in hand, confirming each other in perfect alternation. It was possible to push the collective shadow ever farther off through the process of exclusion, just as it happened with the Indians.

This process gave birth to more than just a new society. It also brought into being the first collective soul that would not compromise with the shadow.

However much the American founders were aware that the Union could victoriously compete with the European powers, they preferred to avoid the issue altogether. Contact with power games would only soil their hands.

No other people that came before them had thrust the contaminating shadow so far away from themselves. Evil was first projected onto England and its monarchy. Then—continuing the English tradition of the "Black Legend" by constructing a negative myth shored up by gossip as much as by history[11]—the black shadow was cast onto Spain, and gradually spread over all the Spanish-speaking Catholic countries. America's political officialdom sought to construct a geography that suited this projection. The Monroe Doctrine (the Annual Message to Congress of December 2, 1823) has been analyzed numberless times as a political manifesto. What ought to interest us as well is its significance as a psychological manifesto, in which the tendency toward purity becomes global. The Americas will remain democratic, while the rest of the world will fall under the shadow of geography and history. Before there was an Iron Curtain (where the ocean was the wall), this doctrine anticipated the psychology of the Cold War.

But the Americas embraced many peoples, whom it was not possible to "purify" by relocation, as with the tribes of Native Americans. The relationships with these peoples could not be avoided. The "Big Stick" of Teddy Roosevelt had not yet been named, but it already leaned against the frame of the Open Door. Along with foreign policy successes in an expansive political program came a failure in political psychology; that failure followed from the psychic tendency toward "purity," which had given shelter to splitting and division.

In a certain sense, American armed forces—in accord with America's absolute historical exceptionalism—have always carried out "police actions." An army can either be victorious or suffer defeat. A police battalion, on the other hand, makes no room for anything except victory. Its only contingencies concern the different possibilities for timing and the measures to be taken. This view of the American military has stripped its enemies of legitimacy and transformed military campaigns into attempts at destroying the shadow: the dark wilderness of the Native American tribes, the darkness that has corrupted many Latin-American regimes, the imperial blackness of international Communism. Ultimately, for the Europeans the two World Wars were wars, but for the USA they were first of all global police actions aimed at defeating outlaw regimes explicitly defined as such.

Only the Civil War was a military undertaking in the full sense of that term: it was witnessed and endured directly by the civilian population, and it called the country's boundaries into question and placed the country in mortal danger. Since the outcome was not the defeat of a national enemy, but rather the preservation of the country's original unity, memory of the war has not nurtured the myth of a good nation that defeats evil ones, but the myth of *a unity that vanquishes division.*

The psychological history of the tendency to purge oneself of shadow accounts for events in American history better than political history does. In contrast to all other countries, the United States has carried out the greater part of its territorial expansion through monetary purchase, even when this was apparently unnecessary, the territory in question having already been acquired by conquest. There is no need to explain this as a calculated move. Naturally, the payment signifies a contractual acceptance of new frontiers, making it more difficult to put them back into question. But from the psychological point of view, making a payment furthers the intention to purify the soul: even if the acquisition was accomplished through an act of violence, that act is projected into the distance, into a past that is already over with and has been replaced by a present based on economic relationships. If a particular affair has been tidied up and finished, it is better for both parties. At the price of *dividing time into distinct epochs*, division is foisted off onto the enemy.

In recent years, Colin Powell has frequently been portrayed in the mass media as an exponent of the strategy of "overwhelming force," as a commander who has prepared not so much for a single military campaign as for total supremacy, a way of fighting that guarantees victory. In reality, this massive superiority is simply the military tradition of the USA. Other conditions being equal, the Puritan tradition is hostile to engaging in any war that continues the confrontation with the enemy, after victory has been secured, in the form of a protectorate, an occupation, or political arrangements that link victors and vanquished in contentions over maintenance of control. In this respect, the unconscious of the radical Protestant tradition fears anything that brings about contamination through continuous contact with the shadow. The adversary—whether military or internal—must not only be conquered but eliminated. Let us not forget how the initials in General U. S. Grant's name came to be read: *Unconditional Surrender* Grant. The two World Wars were no exception,[12] and the American delay in entering them can be explained, in part, as the need to make sure of having maximum superiority when doing so.

This approach comes with a manifest advantage and a hidden cost. If the American tradition unconsciously wishes—at the expense of using either military or economic force—to avoid contamination by shadow, in time it will allow itself to be contaminated by force. Force will become part of the collective shadow; few countries have had as many former generals become president as has the USA. The fact that this has not led to the destabilization of democracy constitutes one of the miracles of American life. However, the United States has defended itself against internal division at the cost of the accumulated envy and ill will of many other countries.

We have in mind not the political but the psychological program, which has been beautifully expressed in the remarkable piece of propaganda from World War II, *Why We Fight*.[13] At the beginning, after focusing on the territories held by the fascist regimes, the camera pulls away into a wide-angle view that finally takes in the whole earth. The viewer is left with a luminous American hemisphere, in contrast to the dark Old World, in every sense immersed in shadow. The story is one of global conflict, but the myth is that of the Monroe Doctrine, an archetype of purity nearly unaltered by time.

The internment of American citizens of Japanese origin during World War II, removing them from the three western coastal states to detention camps, was a further expression of the need to repel the shadow. Very simply, the Japanese are more easily identified as a group, and the psychological cost of constantly seeing the shadow nearby seemed intolerable. One must distinguish, however, between internment and relocation camps. The actual number of internees included a modest majority of German and Italian Americans, along with others of Eastern European descent, next to a large minority of Japanese. The Old World enemy shadow, then, apart from the racial shadow, was sent to barracks in Crystal City, Texas and Fort Lincoln, North Dakota, and even detained at Ellis Island for nearly two years after the war.[14]

In Europe, and particularly in the Catholic countries, it is difficult for people to understand how the practice of capital punishment can enjoy such widespread support in a democratic country such as the USA. One comes to think that state-sponsored violence has habituated Americans to view violence as a normal, daily occurrence. But the historical experiences of the two continents are quite different. In America, capital punishment has been the action of local seats of power, individual state governments, or even sheriffs in small outposts where they represent the only law at hand. In taking that route, the collective unconscious plays out, although in a juridical fashion, the ancient ritual of the scapegoat and its corresponding expulsion of the shadow.[15] In Europe, however, capital punishment has represented the maximum form of deterrence and arbitrary jurisdiction by non-democratic powers. One of the typical formative texts read by my generation was called *Letters from the Resistance by Those Condemned to Death.*[16] For years, the European continent was sealed off by the forces of Nazi fascism, and those condemned to death were condemned politically. In the collective unconscious of Europe, the abolition of capital punishment and the abolition of tyrannies are one and the same thing.[17] At the dawn of the modern West, these positions were reversed. In representing the American Revolution, Thomas Paine gave two speeches (on the 15th and 19th of January 1793) at the French National Assembly, futilely pleading that the former king, Louis XVI, not be put to death.[18]

This quick survey of the relationship between violence and the Puritan splitting-off of the shadow would not be complete without a brief mention of the significance given by the United States to the idea of Social Darwinism[19] and the concept of Manifest Destiny.[20] Social Darwinism was one of the most dangerous of all ideologies (its final fruit in Europe was Nazism), but it attained great popularity in being presented as a *science*—anticipating sociology, anthropology, and genetics.

These two ideological gods were able to sink roots into the American collective unconscious because they were, in several respects, a secular and extremist transformation of Puritanism. Those who are destined to be God's Elect become the darlings of both nature and history. Thus, the idea of superiority was no longer placed in check by Judeo-Christian compassion. The problem of the shadow became more intricate through social complexities: immigration brought into the USA ever fewer Anglo-Saxons and ever more people from Eastern and Central Europe, and over time even more non-Europeans. The Puritan distortion did not really disappear, but slid into the unconscious, while the new "science" inherited the responsibility for housecleaning and decontamination. Evolution seemed to guarantee that the "inferior" races would be wiped out. Assisting in this transformation had nothing to do with moral choice, because the sheer weight of evolutionary conditions was to blame. No individual was violent—no, it was "natural" evolution, with which one could collaborate.

Social Darwinism led people to believe that things were arriving at a stage very near the summit of progress, so that social progressives, paradoxically, were often pushing in this direction more than were conservatives. One example would be those who, following the Civil War, wishing to provide a solution to the problem of the African-

American population, promoted the return of the Blacks to Africa. On the one hand, they were looking for some kind of generous action, one that would alleviate guilt over the institution of slavery. On the other hand, the unconscious fantasy was probably that of freeing themselves from the African shadow (therefore the unconscious double meaning in the name "Liberia").

As one moves through the various levels of exclusion or removal of the weakest, one finally comes to 20th-century eugenics. During the first few decades of the century this practice underwent a powerful expansion throughout the West, but made a particular name for itself in America, whence it would return to Europe, supporting the birth of Nazi ideology.[21]

Psychology and a New Ethic

Jung's disciple Erich Neumann, observing that the victors over Nazism were mounting the threat of nuclear weapons, wrote a short book in 1948 that proposed a *new ethic*.[22] The grounds for this step span several boundaries. The Judeo-Christian tradition appeared to be increasingly less adapted to a technological mass society; the distinction between good and evil had passed directly from religion over into politics. The refusal to recognize that evil was a part of one's own psychology, and the projection of this rejected evil onto the opposing group, transformed the moral distinction into one more instrument of intolerant and implacable struggle. Technical progress—and ideology, which as Solzhenitsyn has said, becomes in its turn the multiplier—changed conflict into extermination.

The only real alternative to catastrophe was the way of psychology. This meant two things. First of all, it was necessary to confront the problem of good and evil on individual terms; condemnation of the group is not a distinction between good and evil but an evil in itself. Second, if a good intention can produce violence, conscious understanding of one's intentions is not enough. The responsibility for violence cannot be suppressed. If, between two adversaries, the party responsible for the violence is always "the other," that other is not to be found in the enemy but in the unconscious. The new ways of proceeding along this path—into the individual person and into what is unconscious—render evaluation and judgment much more difficult. But there is no other alternative. Collective justice has executed far too many injustices.

We have returned to what we proposed at the outset. The opponent, the adversary, the enemy is within us. The recognition of that truth makes one sad.

Walter Benjamin has described the experience of melancholy as the suffering of history.[23] History is a carpet woven out of devastations and assassinations, upon which rides the chariot of the conqueror in triumph. Whoever wishes to understand Carthage must go into mourning. In an act of prudential wisdom, the Romans stood another man next to the triumphant conqueror in his chariot, a double or "other," whose task it was to whisper into his ear that he was mortal, and that successes come and go like the wind.

In the history of my own country, the Roman Empire declared a *Pax Romana*, paid for with slavery and massacres. What followed was a drunken binge, from which we have had to purify ourselves. The voice of the shadow in the chariot was right. During the fourteen centuries that followed the empire, we were divided and subject to foreign domination. It is time to get used to feeling the weight of history and its responsibility, time to grow sad and a bit reasonable.

Could it be that one of America's problems is that the carpet of victims beneath its wheels is still too fresh, that its triumph is still rolling along, and that the excitement arising from all this has not had a chance to subside into melancholy? The heart of America is submerged in the center of history. And so we come to the impossible question: Is it possible to be powerful and just at the same time?

From the psychological viewpoint, the ideas of Social Darwinism and Manifest Destiny are attempts to escape the horror of history and the necessity of struggle. Just as there came a time when people cried *It's God's will!* while sharpening their swords for the Crusades, so these ideas proclaimed: *Science has spoken!*—which is at once the modern god and the new sword.

Should we be at ease because these things took place in the past? I don't know. One recent important book by Peter C. Whybrow, *American Mania: When More is Not Enough*,[24] analyzes the tendency—global, but particularly advanced in America—always to want more while obtaining less satisfaction. This addiction is related to the one we call consumerism, but is especially visible in relation to food, because it leads to obesity. The analysis of this pathology—and of the business that exploits it—is persuasive. The causes, however, can all be explained entirely by way of genetics, or so runs Whybrow's argument: today's Americans are descendants of particularly audacious people, passionate about new things and remarkably insatiable, so much so that they chose to make the great leap across the ocean. In Darwinian terms, the genes for these characteristics were selected and passed down to their descendants.

Since I am not a biologist, it is not my place to take issue with Whybrow's conclusions. But it seems to me that African Americans have a tendency to obesity no different from that among Whites, even though they are not descended from anyone who crossed the Atlantic by choice. I ask myself whether Whybrow is not succumbing to that fear of history that is a trademark of the modern collective unconscious. When we look at ourselves in the mirror, we can scarcely believe what we have become as individuals and peoples, and we prefer to flee from psychological and cultural responsibility into biological explanations.

Just as with the sentencing of a single person to capital punishment, so too with war (which condemns a collective to death): in Europe it could be decided by rulers,[25] while in the United States it has had to gain public approval.[26] A book such as *Just and Unjust Wars: A Moral Argument with Historical Illustrations*[27] is therefore profoundly American and civic in its aim of discussing when a war is moral. But can war, today, be moral?

The ethic that sets out to talk about a just war—and not *inevitable* war, or war *justified by the absence of alternatives*—is, unfortunately, still the old collective ethic, seeking some kind of collective punishment. Technical progress has multiplied atrocities almost beyond limit. At the end of the 19th century, war unavoidably killed civilians, but at least 90% of the dead were soldiers. Things rapidly reversed themselves between World War I and World War II: in World War I, there were 8.6 million military casualties and 6 or 7 million civilian victims. In Word War II, there were 17.1 million military compared with 20 to 27 million civilian deaths.[28] Today, the majority number reverses the earlier ratio exactly: 90% of the dead in our wars are civilians.[29]

The American military today has the ability to avoid, and indeed a preoccupation with avoiding, civilian casualties, more so than any military organization in human history. Notwithstanding this, if we are mindful of the massacres in Iraq, we must conclude that in modern warfare the slaughter of innocents is no longer a chance or collateral occurrence, but the unavoidable essence of conflict.

A central criterion for evaluating war is the proportionality between war aims and human costs.[30] If the human costs of war today cannot be controlled by the authorities who decide to wage war, then we must reconsider the very idea of the just war, because the ones who make the decision can no longer know what they are doing or evaluate it properly, and therefore cannot actually authorize it. What Erich Neumann has called a new ethic demands of anyone a personal assessment, and Odysseus already knew that this calls for *time*. The psychic processes of the unconscious cannot be accelerated.

In this respect, the memoirs of Traudl Junge—who was Hitler's personal secretary from 1942 until the dictator's suicide in 1945—are instructive and excruciating. What she learned little by little during the years following the war, and narrates in her memoirs, is frightening enough. But she had to live through another half century in order for the most tremendous thing to come home to her—that much time was required to portray to her fully the evil that she had encountered and with which, even if in a minimal way, she had collaborated.[31] Her adversary, the person she most despised, was not some crude Nazi, but the girl whom she herself had been. Slowly, Traudl Junge had accomplished the ethical *personalization* that Neumann describes.

She was trying to forgive herself for saying to herself that she was too young at the time to know what was going on. One day, on the street, she saw a monument to Sophie Scholl, one of the young people martyred in the White Rose resistance to Hitler.[32] Reading the inscription on the monument, she found out that she and Sophie had been the same age, and that in the same year that she began working for Hitler, Sophie had been sentenced. She realized that the fact of not being informed about evil and not consciously choosing it does not take away responsibility. She discovered another person within herself, an accomplice, by omission, to assassination. She also discovered that we become morally divided within ourselves over the course of time. Perhaps this fact already invalidates capital punishment: even the worst criminal, given time, is able to become a just man. By taking such a man's life, we also kill that just man who probably has begun to grow in him but might still be in the infant stage.

Hitler, Junge tells us, was directly moved when he sensed that certain of those who carried out his orders felt compassion for the victims. "You understand," he told them, "that it is necessary to sacrifice one's feelings for the common good. When everyone comes to see the results, they will understand that it was worth the suffering. In the meantime, you must not feel guilty, I assume the responsibility." These are the collective norms of the old ethic. Someone takes on the charge of evaluating things for us, of deciding if war is just, or if eugenics—of which genocide is the extreme manifestation—is a good thing. Naturally, war and eugenics are collective operations and demand collective judgments; but the assessment is collective because it is functional, not because it is moral.

I go in fear of that adjective "just." It is something far too lofty to be pressed into service by something as base as war. It becomes dangerous, like an explosive device. It transforms a murderous impulse into something acceptable. What a strong temptation that is, just as strong as the one to obey those people who say they know what the collective good is and take responsibility for it. They seem generous twice over, because they busy themselves with the good of the collective and even offer to carry the charge of our conscience. They offer us inner calm, untroubled by division.

It becomes easier to kill when this kind of inner agreement prevails. And still easier, if one can say—with Shakespeare's King Richard III—that even one's enemies

> Had rather have us win than him they follow.
> ... If you fight against God's enemy,
> God will, in justice, ward you as his soldiers.
> If you do sweat to put a tyrant down,
> you sleep in peace, the tyrant being slain.
>
> —*Richard III*, Act V, Scene 3, ll. 198-210

I do not know with any certainty whether killing is ever justifiable. I do know, however, that no one ought to sleep in peace after having taken a life.

CHAPTER TWO

Trauma and Abuse: The Development of a Cultural Complex in the History of Latin America

> Oh! Before this moment, I existed. My heart is mortally wounded.
>
> —*Codice Fiorentino*, Book VI

In Mexico, as nowhere else, the encounter between natives and Europeans takes the shape of trauma and collapse for the pre-existing society. While the war against the Incas and their empire lasted forty years and the campaign against the Mayas almost a century and a half, the one against the Aztecs was over in less than two years, by 1521, and much less than that if one counts only the period of effective military engagement. It seems that the Spaniards, penetrating a vast and forbidding region whose language and geography they did not know, spent most of their time on foot, dragging their heavy supplies.

In no other place does such a cataclysm defy explanation by normal logic. The Aztec empire, besides being large and highly organized, relied primarily on its military invincibility. It was also a young state in full expansion, far indeed from being decadent. On the other hand, from the viewpoint of myths and archetypes there are no surprises. For in no other place does such a social collapse yield so readily to internal explanation. Prophecies, rituals, and transcendent beliefs: everything prepares the Mexicans to renounce not only armed struggle but also the survival of their own identity once the Spaniards arrive.

Perhaps in no other place (and here the "perhaps" is necessary because the reconstruction is entirely psychological) does the identification of a whole people with an emperor (because of his absolute role as well as the almost complete identity between politics, astrology, and myth) seem to have induced psychic contamination of society as a whole by disseminating his personal collapse through its fabric.

Nowhere else, finally, and at no other time in history, have collective depression and renunciation of the will to live (when not an explicit will to die) so plainly led to a people's cultural and nearly physical disappearance (with the help of hunger, disease, and massacre, of course). According to some calculations, by the end of the 16th century—the century of the conquest—the native population went from 25 million to 1 million, a survival rate of 4 percent, and shrank to less than 3 percent during the two decades that followed. That corresponds to the disappearance of over 97 percent of the entire subcontinent's population.[1]

That is, something has broken, very high up; it doesn't matter whether in heaven or in Montezuma's personality, because the heavens reach down to the common man through Montezuma and the priests who surround him. And the distance separating the common man from Montezuma is infinitely greater than the one separating Montezuma from heaven. This rupture was communicated to the whole people as a process of contamination, one that although not instantaneous certainly worked very fast—if it is true that Montezuma was in fact killed by his own deranged followers.

What interests us here is the fact that this deep wound remains open throughout the following centuries. It even goes on to serve as the basis for national identity—one that can be said to have fused with a cultural complex. This negative identity, sour and repressed, was described by Octavio Paz in one of Latin America's most famous essays, "The Labyrinth of Solitude."[2] The violence of this negative identity forcefully struck me, as a European visitor, at the National Museum of Anthropology in Mexico City. This museum is built upon that fracture, but in such a way that the cleavage remains implicit and is never named. Everything simply stops with the arrival of those vessels from Europe. That is, the National Museum of Anthropology itself conveys the idea that those vessels, and Europe with them, play no part in the gradual formation of the Mexican *anthropos*. One has no notion of what they are; they are something other—excessively "other." The museum visitor is led to sense that Mexico's anthropology and the Mexican nation are to be grasped only in that fracture, that those Spanish vessels, aiming to trespass a frontier, instead brought the frontier with them. It has installed an unbridgeable split between past and present, a flagpole of otherness stuck in the heart of Mexico.[3]

History and Linearity

If the European visitor is as ignorant as I am, the deep disturbance he feels at this revelation may prompt him to get in a car and drive north, to visit Teotihuacan and the nearby monastery of Acolman. There he will traverse a peaceful pre-Columbian town and Catholic religious center. In doing so, he will hope to unite both worlds, at least in his own personal experience. But he will fail. The fracture becomes deeper when one visits places such as this one, which compresses into one narrow space a Spanish church and a pre-Hispanic archeological site. We find in fact two opposite conceptions of time facing each other, never to be reconciled: the time of the natives and the time of the conquerors. Circular time and linear time.

Native time is alternation, rotation, and the return of the stars, the gods, and also of certain events that are known in advance because they are inseparable from those higher powers. The conquerors' time seeks perfection, is assigned to willpower, and has been codified in a sacred text, but such time proceeds without ruptures into secular modernity: its thrust supports the craving for individual improvement and the collective construction of history that typifies the peoples of the Bible and the Western world.[4]

The circular conception of time is known to us thanks chiefly to the work of Mircea Eliade,[5] who related it to simpler populations and their dependence on agricultural cycles. Mexican society represents something much more complex, but its idea of time remains obsessively bound to an original moment in which everything was already predicted.[6] Because everything is contained in that originating cosmogony, everything has been decided and made sacred by it. With no concept of history and becoming, no effective writing system to register it, and no sacred text from which to seek guidance, the Aztecs do not overcome the idea of the eternal return; they transfer this "primitive" concept to a level of complexity more in accord with their society and religion. To know what is right and wrong, what should and should not happen, it is not enough to know the year and its agricultural cycles, for those in turn nest within the cycles of the years and the stars. In this framework, everything becomes predictable and unchangeable because it has been foreseen, or at least minutely prearranged, in the past. But such knowledge is not accessible to the common man—being restricted to priests, astrologers, and elders (since the Aztec "year" corresponds to 52 of our years)—and is cultivated by obsessive repetition and canonical ritual (with literal recitation of the ancient truths, which form the core education of the young).

Tzvetan Todorov[7] has lucidly demonstrated the relationship between the absence of a sacred written text and the craving for continuity through oral repetition, which presupposes the recurrence of certain basic events. It seems to us, however, that the lack of writing actually reveals something much deeper and more widespread: a pre-existing anxiety that is not caused solely by the absence of writing.[8] That lack simply exposes a deeper factor. Since the Aztecs could not rely on writing as an external registry of the past or the passing seasons, as in other cultures, their craving for continuity and collective identity[9] had to be expressed in a frenzy that we can hardly imagine.

But let us try nonetheless. Surrounded by the ruins of Tula, Montezuma tries to listen to the voices of stones, which whisper to him old tales about the greatness of the Toltecs, who were there before the Aztecs: the obsession with the return of the god Quetzalcoatl is not only part of a fixation on that greatness, but also an absolute need for revival of the past. There is no identity without the permanence of what has been. Furthermore, there is no existence without permanence. Since continuity cannot be found in outer records—written texts—it is sought in an inner, mental record; that is, in that part of psychic experience that we call archetype. In the absence of outer means of continuity, the decisive factor is the psychic experience whereby all that is already known will one day return. That experience becomes the single truth.

The surviving Aztec wise men, forced to confront Franciscan friars, would not think of entering into theological debate, something inconceivable to them. Displaying great modesty, they would not argue in favor of their own religion. They would simply say that it had always been the way it was. Their faith was identical with that of their parents and their forebears; the reassuring experience of the archetype repeating itself offered proof of their religion's validity, not the other way round. Aztec religion is not a theological system, but an experience of archetypal emotion that one cannot confute with abstractions. And if this religion is experienced archetypally, its essential outward manifestation will take place where the great archetypes are projected: in dreams and visions to which a prophetic value is attributed, or in astrology.

For Montezuma, the arrival of the Spaniards ruptures that continuity which ruled the world. For him, the strangeness of the newcomers is not the inconceivable aspect. Even if horseman and horse were taken as a single being, what would be so inconceivable about that? Just call them gods and everything becomes reasonable; the Aztecs were used to even stranger gods. The inconceivable factor is that their arrival instituted a *novum* and not a repetition. A new-type rather than an archetype. Thus, Montezuma's first concern is not to know what will happen next, but to discover what has already happened. He frantically consults elders all over the empire. He stops only when he finds one who possesses ancient drawings that depict similar beings: proof that the Spaniards' arrival was predicted—in fact, actually foreseen.

We are unable to examine those pictures, but even so, we are not convinced that they resembled the newcomers: for instance, some of those figures were said to be riding eagles instead of horses. However, we are convinced that Montezuma had found exactly what he wanted: not explanation, but pre-existence; not resemblance, but archetype; not *veri*-fication (that is, the substantiation of truth), but the emotion of continuity.[10]

We realize, in studying Montezuma's biography, that his frightened surprise in the face of radical novelty was the first traumatic rupture of his life. At this point we take another step, beginning to link the general notion of rupture with that of psychological trauma—not personal trauma, however, but a collapse of the Aztec psyche as a whole. This event reminds us that a common myth, an archetype that appears in many different cultures, is precisely the marker of rupture: the archetype of catastrophic event that disturbs cosmic order and puts the world in danger, driving it off its axis.[11] The regular rotation of the cosmos is interrupted, and its axis tilts dangerously.

If for Montezuma the meeting of the two hemispheres amounts to a disturbance of the world's axis, for the Spaniards the same meeting corresponds to its reorientation according to the Treaty of Tordesillas of 1494: a perfect vertical line, and perfectly new. Like all perfect verticals, this one ideally unites earth and heaven—and what else should we expect, since it issues from the infallible Pope?[12]

This readiness to cut the world in two with the blessings of God seems to us something modern and profane, not so much for its materialism as for its capacity to remain undisturbed in the face of absolutely new events and even to take hold of them. This capacity seems to have left behind the sense of continuity based on archetypal repetition. The conquest concerns *new* lands. Yet this readiness belongs mainly to men devoted to action, to adventurers who will increasingly dominate the world; under the surface, the majority of Europeans still need archetypes, and that makes them not so different from Montezuma. A clear example would be the Valladolid debate of 1550, at which the proper treatment of subdued native populations was discussed. The confrontation placed Bartolomé de Las Casas, who is known to have dedicated his life to defending the Indians, against Gines de Sepulveda, who stood for a point of view that today would be called imperialist. Las Casas won the debate, although centuries of oppression may have caused us to forget this. It is not the conflict between good natives and evil Europeans that history registers, but the starting point of that uninterrupted debate which eventually led to secular, complex, and pluralist Western society. We can pass without interruption from those apparently naïve debates to today's theology of liberation and international law.

Those debates were exemplary because of what the opponents implicitly agreed upon. Las Casas espoused the view that an event such as America's discovery should have been announced in the sacred scriptures.[13] Sepulveda, who advocated radical submission on the part of the Indians, invoked the authority of Aristotle (who described the archetype, so to speak, of enslavement in his *Politics*). Both Las Casas and Sepulveda tried to prove their vision of truth by maintaining that it corresponded to an ideal and pre-existent model, and was therefore eternal.

Friar Bernardino of Sahagún, to whom we owe an extensive work dedicated to preserving Aztec memory, in his turn followed Gioachino da Fiore's utopian prophecy of the coming Age of the Holy Spirit, choosing to "read" the meeting between Europe and America as the sign that the new era was dawning. Even those like Sahagún, who dedicate themselves to history, the most characteristic result of human action, insist upon inserting events in a chain of necessary, inevitable, and long foreseen recurrences. For Christians, too, it is the fact of having been prefigured and *announced* that makes Christ Christ. A central trait of the Western world is the intertwining of history's mundane character—that man is free to live day by day, without divine intervention—with certainties, truths, and pre-existent prophecies. Not even Marxism has escaped the influence of this tradition.

Trauma and Abuse

We remember Hamlet's utterance, "The time is out of joint. O cursed spite, / That ever I was born to set it right." When the axis of his world gets out of joint, Montezuma feels that a similar malediction has fallen upon him. Much like Hamlet—to whom he, during his phase of enigmatic uncertainty, has been compared—Montezuma, head of the army and the empire, becomes depressed, anxious, apathetic, and hesitant. Like Hamlet, Montezuma is alone; and like Hamlet, he is still respected, yet feels that others plot against him. Unlike Hamlet, however, he has no recourse to autonomous, secular thinking: all is magic, prophecy, and prescribed deed.

In Montezuma, astrology blends with a certain "historical" knowledge of his own society. Knowing how recent the Aztec state is, he wants to strengthen it by emphasizing his descent, in the maternal line, from the vanished Toltec state. Montezuma must have had in his hands the illustrated pre-Colombian text that we know as *Codex Windobonensis.* This document tells the story of the Toltec god Quetzalcoatl, who for the Aztecs was a secondary deity, the feathered-serpent god who, disappearing *in illo tempore,* has generated the morning star or Venus, and one day will return, coming from the East. According to most accounts written soon after the conquest, the Spanish landing was preceded by many prophecies of doom for the Aztec empire. Abiding by those texts, Montezuma would have immediately interpreted Cortes's arrival as Quetzalcoatl's return, and largely in accord with them would have treated the Spaniards as gods. We do know that around 1550 the belief had spread among subdued, disoriented, and humiliated Mexicans that the Conquest had been announced. But we do not know to what extent those prophecies were known *before* the Conquest, or if Montezuma believed in them in 1519. It may be meaningful, however, that the oldest of those sources—the *Tlatelolco Annals,* written by an anonymous Indian living there in 1528—does not mention this at all. It is also clear that Cortes did all he could to endorse this belief retroactively, which provided an inexorable and religious basis for his power.

Enter again our step of making the link to trauma. From a psychological point of view, this belief could have been disseminated gradually following the defeat—a possibility that Todorov, too, leaves open[14]—and supported by the Spaniards, who exerted growing control over information. The Mexicans, in turn, might have tried unconsciously to elaborate on the trauma, re-establishing its transcendent meaning and reconnecting their mythic and circular time to the historical and linear time into which they had been forcibly thrown.

Also from a psychological point of view, Montezuma's personal behavior might have resulted from trauma. He seems in fact to dissociate into contrasting attitudes. On the one hand, he sends gifts and ambassadors to honor the arrival of the new gods; on the other, he sends magicians to annihilate them with spells. According to certain sources,[15] he even combines his contradictory attitudes into a single act: he sends word to the Spaniards that he will offer them whatever gift they wish if they will refrain from seeing him. (Naturally, in so doing, he excites their cupidity and provokes the opposite effect.) The magicians declare that their arts are powerless, and this too may have strengthened Montezuma's belief that he was dealing with real gods.

To the extent that Quetzalcoatl's return galvanizes attention and obscures the sense of events, Montezuma's magical thinking persuades him that the world is sick and that its axis—to use Santillana's image—may have been shattered already *in illo tempore* with the god's disappearance. In that case, the very return of the god in Spanish dress may have restored the god to his rightful place. The effort to exorcise the newcomers is no military tactic: against a few hundred Spaniards, Montezuma could have sent hundreds of thousands of warriors, but he hesitates too long. The battle, on the contrary, is a mental one. Montezuma tries to squeeze the new event into an old mold, to reintroduce historical time into cyclical time, and to transform the invasion of Cortes—who was in Mexico for the first time—into the idea of return. That being the state of affairs, time will still belong to the Aztecs, although the land will belong to the returning god. Montezuma therefore exchanges land for time, selling out the sovereignty of a country for that of a sacred calendar. But the calendar soon proved to be useless without a country.

Too many things were not predicted by the Aztecs, and the "return of the gods" became meaningless. The deities arriving on the vessels showed themselves increasingly to be brutal, greedy, and mean. Among the new facts, these proved to be determinative. In the end, Mexicans no longer called the Spaniards gods, but *popolocas,* a word that means more or less the same as "barbarians." The new event was truly novel and could not be poured into pre-existing molds.

So why could Montezuma not make up his mind about a coherent, organized military defense? Again, the explanation can only be a psychological one. All our sources describe Montezuma as growing more and more depressed, anxious, and apathetic. Instead of living the conflict externally, which would be true to form for a warlord, he internalizes it to the point of paralysis. By then Montezuma may have had his doubts about the divinity of Cortes, but inside the emperor's soul an omnipotent creature, a deadly and monstrous god, had already taken root. Montezuma had been duped, imprisoned, and abused, yet he went on vacillating between attempts at ineffective reaction and efforts at ingratiating himself with the Spaniards by concessions or gifts. Montezuma—and through osmosis probably an increasingly large number of his subjects—acted like someone who has suffered the most catastrophic of traumas: abuse by a person whom he had trusted without reserve.

The traumatized Mexicans may have experienced a wounding even more lacerating than that of parental abuse and betrayal: *they had been abused by their gods.* All the subsequent symptoms correspond to this original catastrophe and remained petrified for centuries in generations of descendants: a loss of self-confidence and initiative, an introjection of conflicts without any visible sign of aggressiveness, and inclinations to both self-destructive behavior (addiction, suicide) and re-enactment of the abuse. In effect, this trauma constellated a cultural complex in the Mexican psyche. It has all the hallmarks of a complex, whether personal or cultural. It remains largely unconscious; it expresses itself in powerful moods and repetitive behavior; it collects new experiences that confirm its pre-existing, historical experience of the world; and it is autonomous, living a relatively uninterrupted life in the unconscious, where its engine fires according to its own rules and timing. Finally, it tends to activate its bipolar opposite in North American and European "others," who can rapidly and unconsciously fall into the cultural complex by looking and feeling like Cortes.

If a trauma is ever to be brought out and reassimilated, this happens through the laborious examination and innovation that are characteristic of linear, not cyclical, time. The Mexican emperor's fixation on cyclical time was his first self-defeating, masochistic symptom. This trauma, however, is not only an individual event but also an historical one. Accordingly, cyclical time is not only the general form of premodern time, opposed to the European form, but also an individual experience that can persist as an inaccessible island inside our modern world. The cyclical experience of time is actually the regressive container in which we seek refuge after suffering unbearable trauma. As a vicious circle, trauma reproduces precisely the existential conditions that generated it. But now circular, reassuring time no longer corresponds to stability and insertion in a society; on the contrary, it represents isolation and pathology.

Trauma and History

We have not done the customary thing here, which is to focus attention on an historical event in order to amplify a clinical analysis. On the contrary, we have turned to the clinical in hopes of attaining a better understanding of this cataclysm, perhaps the greatest in human history.

According to Donald Kalsched, to whom we owe the only real study of trauma from an archetypal point of view, trauma can be defined as what happens when a negative experience cannot be dealt with through normal psychic defenses.[16] Then a second line of defenses comes into play, which are invincible and archetypal (in the sense that they are not personally elaborated and cannot be personally controlled). They are also demonic, or diabolical, because absolutely autonomous and capable of producing a complete separation—*dia-ballo*, from which we have the word *diabolical*—between the self and the external world. The purpose of such defenses is actually the ultimate and complete protection of the self when it is attacked by something that threatens its psychic survival. But that same defense against an unbearable wound tends to become unbearable in its turn; thenceforth, the faintest sign of danger may evoke the archaic defensive demon. The psyche becomes nearly static, not learning from external experience and no longer interacting with it. The secondary defense resulting from an occasional event becomes the only event. Just as in autoimmune diseases, the defense mechanism has gone out of control and attacks the very organism it is supposed to defend. Likewise on the psychological level, an excess of defense means that someone who has suffered traumatic abuse is ready to commit suicide, if by so doing he can prevent the repetition of trauma or even the mere evocation of it (since it is psychic experience we are talking about).

In general, analysts tend to focus upon individual trauma suffered during childhood. Maybe because it is already an insurmountable event by definition, few occupy themselves with the collective trauma that falls upon adults.[17] But collective trauma that besets both adults and children and is remembered for generations can become the node around which a cultural complex forms. It would be all to the good if analysts became more aware of and concerned with cultural complexes. The fact that we have been able to apply a modern view of trauma such as Kalsched's to an event and a culture that are so remote from us seems to confirm on a collective scale that the psyche reacts to trauma by regressing to an archetypal pattern. Manifestations of the reaction will of course vary individually and culturally. Yet the basic model remains invariable, because this reaction activates psychic layers that are neither personal nor cultural, but archetypal. By the same token, the archetypal pattern may well express itself in either a cultural or a personal complex, or in both.

We are often impressed by the fact that reactions to trauma by highly individual personalities in different historical circumstances can be astonishingly similar. When we think of Primo Levi, Odette Rosenstock, or Hans Mayer (better known as Jean Amery), we think not only of Italian, French, and German survivors of extermination camps, or of three Jewish authors who with tremendous effort transformed their experiences into narrative.[18] Above all, we think of three persons who, in spite of achieving such heroic sublimation, one day obeyed, after so many decades, the command from the demon of absolute defense, and killed themselves.

We know that the abused lose their will to live. And through intuition we can understand why so many Mexicans committed suicide or infanticide, or simply stopped fighting disease during the decades that followed the Conquest. It was not because they did not want to face a life of suffering, which in any case already was the fate awaiting most of them, even under Montezuma. Their problem was not suffering, but the impossibility of psychologically incorporating the abuse practiced by the gods. And just as the defense against the psychic presence of abuse must be at least as large, absolute, and divine as the forces behind the abuse, so too must the defense against remembrance in life be total, even at the cost of defending against life itself.

During the pivotal 16th century, the Aztecs enact their own historical suicide.[19] First came a phase in which extinction was a real threat, due to a combination of organic and psychic pandemics; then, for centuries, the population remained apathetic, as happens with the abused. The demonic archetypal defenses, which averted memories but also vital impulses, had clearly saturated what Jungian psychology calls the cultural unconscious. Nothing assures us that such defenses are restricted only to the individual and therefore cannot spread throughout society.

As we know, the abused forget precisely the things that matter most.[20] This fact helps us to understand what I will call the "Octavio Paz Paradox": that the Mexican people, whose past is the greatest among all the American populations, seem unconscious of this, indeed seem not to have a history.[21]

Agreeing with other researchers, Kalsched tells us that trauma tends to reproduce itself, and that the victim tends to favor occasions for its reproduction. In dreams of abused patients, the demonic archetypal defenses manifest themselves again and again as powerful beings, especially as magical animals dedicated to protecting the self, but which at the same time separate the self from life. Language itself gradually ends up reproducing the experience of this short circuit, inevitably repeated when memories approach consciousness. Primo Levi, for instance, long after his liberation, awoke each morning to the autonomous command: "*Wstavac'*!" (in Polish, "Stand up!"), which he repeats in his writings.[22] Or there is Elie Wiesel's opening in *Night*, which, describing his first night at Auschwitz, interrupts itself and turns linear progression into repetition: "I will never forget that night, the first night in camp that has made of my life a long night, seven times shut. Never. ..."[23] The words "night" and "never" become motifs both haunting and lullaby-like that run throughout his book.

Must we not say that such anguish, enclosed in a vicious circle, and so characteristic of survivors from concentration camps, is the same as that expressed by the Aztecs when facing the Spaniards? "Their lances of iron, it was as if they set things afire. And their spades of steel waved like sea foam. It was as if they clanged their vests of steel, their helmets of iron. And others come, all equally covered with iron ...."[24] Or, when they are ambushed: "Oh, worthy warriors! Oh! Mexicans! Come and help! There, they are dead already, the worthy warriors have perished! They are dead, they were betrayed, they were destroyed! Oh! Mexicans! Oh! Worthy warriors!"[25] We may agree with Todorov that tales in the oral tradition tend to be repetitive as a way of fixing them in memory; but we cannot help noticing that the repetition becomes obsessive precisely when the trauma is described. Such obsessive repetition characterizes not only oral tradition, particularly when a tale of trauma is narrated, but also how a cultural or individual complex behaves in the psyche. Every time the cultural complex is activated, repetitive memory and emotion arise to evoke the primal trauma. Trauma, memory, and emotion recur repetitively and are linked through the cultural complex to archetypal, cultural, and personal levels of the psyche.

Let us now go back one step, to the moment when Cortes and the Spaniards began to behave in ways that were increasingly cruel, ways incompatible with those of a god. Our question sought to identify precisely when Montezuma stopped seeing them as gods. But does this question make sense from a psychological point of view? We observed that at this point the antagonism to Cortes was transferred into the soul of Montezuma, becoming an internal conflict and gradually paralyzing him. Is there any sense in trying to discern whether the emperor believed that Cortes was a man or the god Quetzalcoatl? From a psychological point of view, the iron man Cortes and the feathered serpent Quetzalcoatl both express the demonic archetype activated in the psyche following a trauma, fashioned to protect the self but also isolating it. In the external world, Cortes treated Montezuma in exactly that way: he went on honoring Montezuma as emperor after imprisoning him. Cortes-Quetzalcoatl (that is, the archetypal demon) kept the emperor Montezuma (that is, the self) enchained in autism.

Why should it make any difference to know whether, for Montezuma, the god Quetzalcoatl had really returned? All available sources tell us that, after the arrival of Cortes, Montezuma was dominated by the eternal return of invincible inner monsters: "Oh!" he shouts. "Before this moment, I existed. My heart is mortally wounded."[26] How can we help remembering Robert Jay Lifton's description of the traumatized in Hiroshima, *Death in Life*? From a psychological point of view, what has happened is beyond remedy or repair. It will transmit itself to what remains of Montezuma's life, to the lives of his subjects, and, to an extent that is probably underestimated, to their descendants, in what has become a truly monstrous cultural complex. From that point of view, the mythic, prefigured return of Quetzalcoatl as an outer event is identical with the autonomous, inevitable experience of inner repetition that constitutes trauma and its monsters.

CHAPTER THREE

The Duel and Honor

> More than anything else, chivalry meant the duty to act honorably, even in war .... Honor and shame played an important role in enforcement; the sanction of dishonor for the knight who violated his knightly duties, thus becoming a traitor to chivalry and his knightly vow, was quite effective.
>
> —Theodor Meron, *Bloody Constraint: War and Chivalry in Shakespeare* (1998), "Introduction"

> Honor, first of all, is a refusal: a refusal to make a pact with what is gross, abjectly vulgar, an interested party, or mercenary; a refusal to bend in any way to force simply because it is force.
>
> —Lucien Febvre, "Honneur et Patrie" (1945-1946), Lecture III

The human practice of dueling—basically, among men—is as old as the psyche itself. In fact, it predates the existence of the psyche, for it continues the ritualized combats between male animals in rutting season or when their status in the group must be defined.

One of the great lessons taught by Konrad Lorenz deals precisely with this fact.[1] Animals equipped with tusks, claws, and other such lethal weapons counterbalance their natural drive to attack with an equally natural inhibition. Once the adversary is vanquished, he is not finished off. The fight is ritualized, that is, it is kept within non-destructive limits. Human beings are not endowed by nature with lethal weapons, and therefore are not equipped with corresponding natural inhibitions. But human beings are no longer natural. Their culture has fitted them out with every conceivable kind of armament. If no *cultural* limitation were imposed on human aggressiveness (and on the power drive, its civilized metastatic extension), in the end we would exterminate each other.

Duels and Destruction

These cultural limitations are called rituals, customs, and laws—more specifically, the laws of war. Yet, to take only one question that they raise, are the laws of war an abstract invention of the Enlightenment, or did the Enlightenment together with modernity instead codify and rationalize rituals that limit destructiveness and were already at hand in less conscious guise? Indeed, to judge from the earliest recorded epics, respect for the adversary and the need to frame ritualistically even the most grisly mortal combat seem to have existed from the beginning. These rituals were not specific codes to be followed in the way we follow an instruction manual. Although not consciously transmitted, they were probably universally understood. They corresponded—and still correspond—to archetypal ideas of heroism, fairness, and honor.[2]

Although linked with nobility, honor was not the effortless acquisition that noble rank was, a status that came to aristocrats as their birthright. One must deserve honor, and one can lose it. Honor relates to moral reputation, like honesty, which, not by chance, stems from the same root, the Latin *honos*, whose origin is obscure, but which meant both honor and charge (an honorable charge or office, but at the same time charge in the broad sense, stipulating burden and duty). Significantly, plays on words developed around the term, such as *onus est honos qui sustenit rem publicam* (heavy responsibility is the honor that carries the common good), which survives almost intact in the modern Italian *onori e oneri* (honors and heavy burdens). In fact, honor was evidently so central in classical antiquity that it was spelled with a majuscule, as the god Honor.

War has always been an attempt to exterminate the enemy. Though aristocratic and accomplished poetry, neither the *Iliad* nor the *Aeneid* whitewashes the reality of the conquest of Troy: carnage, genocide, the city a sump of blood, women enslaved and the heads of children bashed against paving stones. Yet three times in the *Iliad*, in Books 2, 7, and 22, the immense panorama of battle halts to display a duel between two heroes. Not only do the principal warriors stop, understandably eager to watch, but so does every other contest on the field, according to rules that, though unwritten, are so rooted in everyone's code of honor that they are grasped immediately by both armies. Just as immediately, these archetypal rules must have been understood by every listener—for let us remember that the *Iliad* was composed for oral recitation. For all its notorious tendency to submerge the main thread beneath a plethora of details, the poem does not bother to waste a line explaining either what the rules of the truce were or how they could be enforced instantly upon such a multitude.

The battle among the warriors is ritualized in the clash of the two champions. Fighting is here self-contained; while it is under way, all other combat must cease. Even the army that had gained the upper hand immediately agrees to cancel its advantage. In that moment, destructiveness is ritualistically contained. The initial duel of the three in the *Iliad* is even cast as an attempt to end the entire war, substituting its outcome for the result of full military engagement.

Why is the winning side ready to give up its advantage? Because warfare in every culture aims at a psychological goal that is higher than any material one. If we set aside such egregious exceptions as the conquest of the American West (in itself not a war but an ongoing process of colonization and settlement accompanied by low-intensity warfare), prolonged wars have always brought to both sides greater material loss than gain. War is not about winning. For both sides in a contest (or at least for their ruling elites) the diffusion of, and identity with, a sense of glory, honor, and heroic conduct is more decisive than obtaining material advantage.

The rules for the war at Troy are unwritten, not only because they concern an oral culture, but also because fairness need not be codified. What governs is simply a noble state of mind. The heroes are noble and the nobles are heroes: no further definition is necessary. The duel must be utterly simple and clear, so that no doubt will arise about its good faith. Heroes have mounts and squires, but the horses are for transport only and the squires step back as soon as the duel begins. The duelists first hurl their spears and then brandish their short swords. Anything more would border on the unthinkable—or at least the unintentional—and would be chalked up immediately to some god's malign intervention.

Even in merciless general combat, honor takes precedence over gain, advantage, or victory. In the *Iliad*'s final scene, Hector is facing Achilles at the gates of Troy. Hector knows that Achilles is stronger, and also knows that he himself is Troy's greatest champion and crown prince. His survival is essential to both his family and his country; from the walls everyone calls to him, pleading with him to withdraw inside the gates. Deviating from the usual heroic treatment, Homer even describes him in the grip of fear: terrified, Hector hears a voice within his soul cry, "Run, take refuge!" Yet not for a moment does he think of seeking safety behind the walls. In itself, that would not be dishonorable, for he and the entire Trojan force do this each night and at every lull in the battle. But in the moment of challenge by Achilles, he must respond accordingly: a duel must be fought on equal terms.

Any other course of action would mean seeking an advantage—and losing all honor. By avoiding a fair fight, the duelist condemns himself to feeling shame for the rest of his life. Seeking advantage, you follow your instinct, yet by following it you fail to distinguish yourself from the animals. Your only choice is to make honor your priority. If you follow instinct, you remain an animal even if you win; if you follow honor, you remain a hero even if you lose.

Cavalry and Chivalry

The role of the horse expands as armies seek greater mobility. In the early Middle Ages, the importance of the mounted warrior reaches its peak, and cavalry becomes chivalry. (Significantly, Italian still expresses both concepts with one word, *cavalleria*; in English one still perceives their common origin in one of the Latin words for horse, *caballus*.) The noble personality's desire for elevation finds physical expression in the higher stance of the rider, apart from any military advantage. Horsemen look stronger and more beautiful than foot soldiers. The chivalric ideal directly continues the Greco-Roman one of *kalokagathía*, of high moral and physical qualities indistinguishably united.

It would be a mistake to suppose that the superior power of mounted troops is the focus for idealization. Two streams converge to refine cavalry ethics and turn it into chivalry: the new Christian vision and the practical necessities of the prince. Christianity teaches respect for the weak, the poor, and the defeated; in their turn the princes deplore their mercenary armies, which jump sides in mid-battle when given a better offer; the princes need a more loyal, idealistic force to ensure their power. Gradually a romantic, chiefly moneyless, aristocracy comes into being, a lower nobility whose prestige and role cannot derive from venerable titles and vast holdings. Their specific treasure is the spirit of chivalry. Partly from education at court and partly from the need to carve a role for itself and win universal respect, chivalry refines the ideals of honor, gentility, generosity, and the *beau-geste*. While this effort often abandons realism for excess, nonetheless, for perhaps the first time in Western culture, the poor, unknown knight-errant surpasses the wealthy prince of renown as an ideal for the whole of society.

The chivalrous Nobody wins a hero's praise; and with that unexpected turn, a precocious democratic idea has begun to penetrate society. Paradoxically, it proves at one and the same time how vital aristocratic tradition is, for democratic and conservative ideals thrive together in this trend, both giving expression to the archetype of the noble and loyal warrior. An archetype can express stability and new creativity at the same time. To be honorable means to be radically faithful—equally to one's master, one's beloved, and one's principles. Honor is unconditional fidelity.[3]

As the ideals of loyalty and honor become fully deployed, not only do the weak and downcast win respect, but also, as has been observed, the whole of chivalry is deeply "feminized."[4] And not only does woman stand at the center of the knight's attention; the harsh soul of the warrior itself seems to undergo softening. While earlier heroes took women as objects or property—either as spouses in marriage or as prizes following a victory—the courtly knight stakes his life for a damsel's honor, often without expecting her even to notice him. Here we face a second paradox: on the one hand, chivalry undoubtedly develops out of masculine ethics; on the other, it foreshadows the modern recognition of femininity and its importance.

In this refinement of gentle feeling and respectful attitudes, the fairness in dueling—whether during a tourney or in actual combat—becomes an extreme, ritualized exigency. Medieval heroic cycles often describe knights who would voluntarily dismount if their adversary had fallen from his horse. They condemned the use of new or improved weapons that allow fighting at a distance.[5]

The noblest, most extreme, and, unfortunately, the most ingenuously idealistic attempt made by the medieval code of chivalry was the one that applied that code to warfare. Reviving the Greek notion from which the idea of nobility derives ("aristocracy" comes from *aristos* or best), the chivalric code proposed to have the best men from one country (for example, twenty or thirty champions called, precisely, the *aristìa*) constitute a formation for doing battle with another such array from the opposing country.[6] In this way, the medievals sought to minimize bloodshed, a supreme desideratum in warfare among Christians. Moreover, whether because the number of fighters was reduced, or because everyone held to chivalric rules as their highest ideal, the practice changed a potential massacre intc something stylized, in fact quite elegant. Instead of a slaughter, the public beheld a ritual tournament: rules and dress became essential, and the whole spectacle, with good reason, was thought to be rather beautiful. In any case, the chivalric tourney cannot be reduced either to a game or to an expedient for the discharge of aggression. It is most likely that behind the beginnings of both the duel and the tournament are religious rituals far older than chivalry.[7] The memory of these practices may be lost to us, but even today we have not altogether lost touch with their sacred character.

The ethical, aesthetic, and ritual ideal of chivalry came to exercise priority over material advantages. This factor directly concerned the terms of actual warfare: before a battle, the commencement of hostilities was delayed until a general with a strong sense of honor made parley with his adversary about the time and place for the engagement. If possible, they selected level, gently rolling terrain that would crowd no one.[8]

Naturally, it was difficult to abide by such elevated principles. The commander of an army who, when sizing up the situation, found himself in an advantageous position could respond either by making no excuses or by looking for them. That, however, is not what is interesting. Every ethical ideal remains difficult to attain. The ethical plane on which a society lives depends not only on its approaches to perfection but also on its attempts to grapple with an ideal. In those cases where a commander failed to renounce the advantages that might fall to him, he struggled internally with *a feeling of shame and dishonor*. That fact, which may well surprise moderns, pertains to our theme. For we are dealing with a feeling that, down the succeeding centuries, has gradually sunk into the unconscious, but which has not vanished altogether. When that ideal is reconstructed, modern man feels obliged to smile at such ingenuousness. Nevertheless, one still recognizes something. And it raises the question of whether, when all is said and done, by staying more ingenuous, people might have been able to stay more moral as well.

The extreme austerity of the Middle Ages fades abruptly with the advent of the Renaissance, yet the honorable duel seems so ingrained in the collective unconscious that it remains intact. One Italian masterpiece of the late Renaissance shows this quite clearly. "*Non vuol Tancredi, che pedon veduto / ha il suo nemico, usar cavallo, e scende*" [Tancredi, who has spotted his adversary on foot, has no wish to use his horse, and dismounts].[9] The poem's protagonist does not hesitate. In such a situation one must leap down without discussion or delay. Once again, the epic does not bother to give the reason for this gesture; the writer, Tasso, evidently assumes that the corresponding code of honor is still intact among his readers. Shame on you if word were to get around that you had preferred advantage over fairness!

Centuries later, Sir Walter Scott, a pioneer in modern fiction at a time when life had become far more practical, nonetheless demonstrates how certain aspects of the literary imagination have not changed. Chivalry and the rules of honor, less present in daily life, seem no less present in the collective mind. The pages of *Ivanhoe* still show an obsession with the fairness of dueling and tournaments. Interestingly for us, they need no explanation to make them understandable to a wide and popular readership. The Disinherited Knight, for instance, refuses to take advantage of his challenger after unseating him, renouncing his hit on the basis of the irregular performance of his adversary's mount. Immediately, he offers his challenger a second chance, the first joust not having taken place on fully equal terms.[10] Loyalty to those terms demands that one start over again straightaway. Such immediacy is again a characteristic inherent in any honorable behavior. "Honor," the great historian Fèbvre reminds us, "is an active force, and a force that affirms itself in action and not in speculation… . It engages right away, totally, without discussion or evasion. Honor waits on nothing. Honor never hesitates."[11]

The Transhistorical Nucleus of Honor

In simple societies, where rules had not yet been codified, let alone written down, honor typically was a moral virtue. In the absence of detailed codes, honor goes to whoever acts openly from a noble motive rather than from the desire for immediate, visible advantage. As social complexity grows and rules abound, honor acquires more complex and decorative aspects among the aristocracy. Positively, honor defines a nobleman's right to distinction, but negatively specifies his duties: an insulted commoner can simply shrug off an offence, whereas a nobleman, if an offender fails to apologize, must risk his life in a duel. The more modern and democratic a society becomes, the more rarefied honor becomes. It is less and less necessary in the fabric of norms and social co-existence.

Modern secular thinking often devalues honor as a frivolous externality, like a medal on some nostalgic reactionary's uniform. Yet honor also has a timeless psychological value, and it becomes even more important where it survives, whether among ordinary citizens who are not tied to complex aristocratic codes, or among notables as a paradigmatic example and inspiration for others.

World War I has settled in the collective imagination as the first instance of utterly pitiless carnage. Probably for the first time a pope sided entirely with Christian principles and with none of the belligerents, calling it a "useless massacre."[12] The dawn of a global industrial world witnessed the first global industrial carnage, in which heroism and pity vanished and killing became a matter of numbers and technology. Yet in reading autobiographical accounts of the war we find that, even in conditions that anticipated the 20th century's later devastating wars and genocides, a sense of honor, fairness, and even gentleness surfaced daily, mitigating even the most senseless cruelties.

It is well known that the first paladins of the air behaved like good duelists. The pilots saluted each other, often renouncing pursuit of a badly hit adversary. But even in the mud and excrement of the trenches, fairness did not totally disappear. The general order to fire on every advancing enemy was often overlooked by the ranks and sometimes even by officers. They sensed that it would have been unfair to pick off some poor guy crawling through no-man's-land with the clear intention of recovering the effects of a dead comrade, or simply checking to see if he was still alive. Trenches were sometimes so close to each other that soldiers often recognized the face of their "own enemy"—the one who *faced* them—and this humanized him. To the dismay of their respective commanders, Austrian and Italian infantrymen would greet each other, congratulate each other for the last action, wish their enemies a Happy Birthday, joke about their officers and the horrible food, or even, at Easter, spontaneously breach the barbed wire and stroll with their adversaries in no-man's-land, exchanging food and tobacco.[13] Court-martial was stipulated for anyone who received the enemy with open arms rather than firearms, yet those simple people on both sides knew instinctively that resurrection could not be celebrated with murder, but only by coming out of the trenches with gifts instead of weapons and inventing a simple ritual. The archaic rule of honor, more powerful than any written command, would oblige the enemy to do the same.

With differing moral qualities we come to different rendezvous, particularly in a modern society. As most of us work in some sort of business, most of us have a daily appointment with honesty. Sincerity comes into play less frequently, but we all have met with certain situations where it is at stake. The encounter with honor has a special quality; it is quite rare, and we usually come across it only once in our lives. That quality somehow belongs to its archetypal, unavoidable nature. And that is probably why its archaic, public nature is still so important, and why it is still associated with aristocratic features: it is the noble—or ignoble—moment of our lives. And rightly so. Something refined, something noble in the original sense of the word, must remain rare, for otherwise it quickly degenerates through inflation and bad taste, just as the excesses of "honor rituals" did toward the end of the Middle Ages.

Maximilian of Hapsburg, a naïve prince, let himself be tempted into a cynical colonial adventure in Mexico. When things turned out badly and France withdrew, he could have re-embarked for Europe. But at that point he identified truly with his role, and refused. He lost both his naïvety and his life, but preserved his honor. And that is how he will be remembered. Manet's paintings of his execution represent exactly that: a timeless exaltation of his honor, not an ephemeral image of obsolete aristocratic values.

At the tragic end of the Nazi-fascist military adventure, two men strove to reach the Swiss border with the routed German army: the head of the collaborationist Vichy regime, Marechal Pétain, and the Italian dictator Mussolini. At the last moment Pétain refused to escape, retracing his steps and handing himself over to a French court, knowing that his only alternatives were life imprisonment or death. He spent the rest of his days in jail and silence. Mussolini thought only of escaping, and disguised himself in the uniform of a simple German infantryman. But he was too well known; at a roadblock some Italian partisans recognized him, and he was executed almost on the spot. He did not even receive the great public trial that his position would have granted him, and so he sinned twice against honor: not only did he not face his adversaries, he also denied the celebrity that he had constantly fought to gain. That radical loss of honor has vaccinated Italy against a resurgence of fascism more than any conditions imposed by the victorious Allies.

American Honor

The USA established the foundations of an absolute democratic society. Of course, the French Revolution also proclaimed universal values, but these did not reach us without interruptions in time (having to negotiate five republics and two empires), and ruptures in space, which European colonization could not overcome, but which American globalization was able to surmount.

No one recognized this fact better than Alexis de Tocqueville, the founder of a comparative ethnology for Western society. It is a coincidence worth mentioning that the notes for Lucien Fèbvre's rich course of lectures on "Honneur et Patrie," which I have been drawing upon, and which he delivered directly after the defeat of Nazi fascism, disappeared after his death in 1956, and were published only forty years later because they had been lost in the attic of Alexis de Tocqueville's castle in Normandy.

From its beginning, the USA has rarefied the existence of honor in modern social conditions.[14] The chief, shadowily persistent function of traditional aristocratic honor was to preserve the sharp differences between social classes. Tocqueville anticipated that this function would fade away with the mobility of American life, and that its relics would show up in ethnic distinctions. Yet the sharp eye of this French aristocrat keenly appraised the kind of honor that indeed has survived in the USA, including its possible future clones. What he saw is that honor would be democratized, gradually leaving behind the traditional military challenge to enter new fields. The rules of honor would become much simpler and the challenges to honor more rare, but not necessarily less important. Provided that everyone works honestly (to be rich and lazy is not enough), everyone is honorable. Departing from aristocratic norms, a certain degree of honorability is taken for granted in each person. The merchant in the East and the settler in the West are assumed to be loyal adversaries. The use of the bank account by one and the revolver by the other are fundamental rights allowed in fair competition.

The public aspect of honor enters a new, democratic phase with the birth of American society. The most famous political document of all time, the Declaration of Independence of the United States of America, calls honor "sacred" and chooses it *as its final word*—as if honor were its seal, and as if it were more important than the signatures. Honor had ceased being a genetically acquired quality of the aristocracy and had been reborn as a preoccupation of the secular politician, in his capacity as a representative of the whole population.[15]

A Modern Tale of Dueling

What Tocqueville did not foresee was that a modern Homer would not only preserve but also canonize the survival of the essential democratic sense of honor. That Homer's name is Hollywood. And in order to create real epics, Hollywood has had to be fully as blind as its Greek predecessor. Of course, not every fight and not every fighter in Hollywood's tales turns out to be fair; no story could survive without surprises and evildoers. But the tale must hint quite clearly at what an honorable fight must be, so that the public will know instantly and instinctively when somebody violates its tenets, and will drown him in contempt.

Thus it is that Hollywood renders honor for the citizen of modern society. At the same time, by stereotyping it for fictional reasons, Hollywood returns honor to its original purity and spreads it abroad again through its global might. Make no mistake, it says, honor remains the priority it has always been.

What challenge, then, what honorable contest takes place every four years like the Olympic Games or the soccer World Cup, but attracts a greater public than the Olympics, the World Cup, and the Americas Cup put together? We all know the answer, of course: the election of the President of the United States. We also know that the 2000 election established a watershed, and not only between centuries and millennia. It also separated the prototype of the honorable duel from something alien, a scuffle that fell to earth from the Planet of the Cheats.

Traditional duels featured seconds and witnesses, and a traditional tournament implied large crowds. Their unstained approval was more important than the outcome of the duel itself. The merest suspicion that the weapons used in the contest were not strictly equivalent would have dishonored any duelist. At the very hint of such suspicion, therefore, he would have turned voluntarily to the table of the seconds, or to the gallery where the regent sat, asking each witness to verify the weapons or to exchange them, renouncing any possibility of unfair advantage, and reclaiming his honor in doing so. Every good-faith fighter has abided by this practice, from the lonely medieval knight to the cowboy of the American Wild West. But in 2000 none of this happened. Did one duelist carry a switchblade and the other a tinware dinner knife? Did one ride a horse and the other a donkey? No one could say, and clearly the duelists themselves did not know. But that is not the point: duelists must be fair, not omniscient.

As uncertainty persisted, a growing unease gripped the nation and eventually the world. Deepening anxiety grew into panic, submerged in the flow of TV and newspaper accounts—a gigantic but pointless flow, without meaning or feeling. The panic did not stem from some vision of the great American democracy grinding to a halt; that was only the gossip of envious Europeans. No, American democracy is an engine that rumbles along ceaselessly, at times mercilessly. Never, not even during the 2000 election, has it stumbled into a power vacuum. As for the economy, it is enough to recall that during the dramatic uncertainty following the election Wall Street performed with amazing stability, beginning to suffer considerable losses only after confirmation of victory by the candidate backed by the major financial interests.

The modern American President has often been described, because of his unrestrained power, as an imperial figure. What we are pointing out here is that, because of the archetypal ritual that took shape with the challenges that led to a president's eventual acclamation, the figure of the president is also heroic.

The year 2000 is still very recent, yet seems so far away, because we repressed a certain profound feeling at that time, and we are repressing its memory now. To repress something means to drive it far from consciousness. At the time, even the best print media and television commentators were able to discuss only technicalities—legal and political niceties—and thereby entirely missed the point. An honorable duelist would have brought his weapons—in this case the ballots that were cast for him—back to the table, and he would have asked to start the duel all over with new weapons: new ballots, new whatever. But precisely there—in archetypal space, not in some political scenario—we entered the vacuum that triggered our panic. Contrary to the heroic archetype that stands behind and supports the presidential figure, we witnessed a duelist who, like some weak street kid, promptly turned to his bigger brothers—the lawyers, the judges—and, rather than bringing his weapons back to the table, asked their help in carrying the table off and declaring as finished a duel that—according to the general, archetypal expectation—had not even begun.

The greatest country in the world—or at least the one that controls the world—was being deprived of the greatest and most perennial of myths, in which a hero keeps faith with his role. The scar from this wound will not quickly or easily disappear from the collective unconscious. At the time critics could only talk about technicalities, while the reins of world power were being entrusted for years to the one person who had proved himself incapable of holding, even for a single day, the reins of honor.

CHAPTER FOUR

Nightmares

The Nightmare and the Invention of the Other

What art thou that usurp'st this time of night?

—Shakespeare, *Hamlet*

One day a man looks out through his eyes and for the first time sees someone else.

He sees that however much he wanted to remain like the other, experiencing his feelings and suffering his torments, the other person would remain ineluctably other. And incomprehensible to him. No longer does he see difference as something that he can hope to incorporate, that is, as a departure from original sameness that although definitive still remains manageable, letting all waters return to one ocean. In this loss of hope he despairs. And he murders his brother.

According to some, that was the day on which the human being forever separated itself from the animal.[1]

And on the day that Cain arrived, so did our theme, the nightmare.

Why, when the human being pulls away from the animal, does the nightmare irremediably attach itself to the dream? By nightmare we generally mean a particular kind of dream, pathological and beyond the normal range. But as soon as we want to know more, our difficulty begins.

Freud named it without defining it. Jung, too, did not deal with the nightmare as such, but he did discuss its etymology,[2] as we shall do further on. Among the pillars of psychiatric learning—Jaspers in the German school, Bleuler in the Swiss, Ey in the French—"nightmare" cannot be found in the analytical indexes to their manuals. The same holds true for the American school in *The Harvard Guide to Modern Psychiatry*, although the classic work of Arieti makes reference to nightmare in the title of his chapter elsewhere on insomnia.[3] He does not, however, speak of insomnia as the collateral effect of nightmares, but of the nightmare as a collateral effect of insomnia. As soon as we turn to it, it walks off, leaving us unfed.

The American Psychiatric Association, whose job it is to classify each and every suspect form of human behavior, gives us this description of nightmare:

> Nightmare disorder: Sleep disorder of the parasomnia group, consisting of repeated episodes of nightmares that awaken the sleeper, who rapidly becomes fully oriented and alert and can vividly recall the dreams. Onset is usually in childhood or adolescence, and children often outgrow the disorder. Called also dream anxiety disorder.[4]

The *Nightmare Disorder* is not defined as a psychiatric one. (In passing, we may ask ourselves whether this description can be called a definition or a tautology: the APA says that the nightmare disorder consists in the appearance of nightmares.)

It is suffered for the most part in infancy, whereas with passing years it goes into spontaneous remission or complete recovery. The data, however, varies even in the USA, which has the largest bibliography in the field.[5] The percentage of American babies affected runs from 10 to 50 percent, and in adults, from 1 to 8 percent. *Nightmare Disorder* is to be distinguished from *Sleep Terror Disorder*, in which the subject has troubled sleep but has difficulty waking up completely and recording the dream. This syndrome, too, in any case, is typical of infancy and diminishes with age. Forming a group by itself are the nightmares linked to certain forms of epilepsy, to *Delirium*, and to *Post-Traumatic Stress Disorder*. The percentages suffering from the most serious post-traumatic disturbances—those resulting from war—likewise vary widely. As we shall see later on, this is also because the classification of disorders varies from war to war. Obviously, too, the frequency greatly varies, depending on the type of conflict; among survivors of the Arab-Israeli War of 1973, 68 percent suffered from nightmares, while among those of the First Gulf War only 1.8 percent did (obviously this figure pertains to the Western allies and not to the Iraqis).

Since the nightmare breaches the levees of sleep and enters another condition, the waking state, the attempt to define nightmare breaks the bounds of medicine and psychiatry (disciplines that study dreams and sleep, replacing religion, which dealt with them in the past) and enters unknown territory. When we look into nightmares, from which scientific perspective should we peer? In the total absence of pre-existing definitions, I believe it is up to us to decide. Therefore, I propose considering the nightmare as a borderline concept, situated in a zone where the boundaries of psychoanalysis, medicine, anthropology, and philosophy meet each other.

The nightmare is a dream that the individual psyche cannot contain. If the "normal" dream newly elaborates and combines archetypal themes—that is, themes that pre-exist the dreamer—with memories deriving from experience, the dream changes into nightmare when the stimuli can no longer be contained and assimilated by the inner world; when the dreamer seeks fruitlessly to rework, in dream images, a conflict that has no inner resolution; or when one can no longer successfully absorb the excess of meaning, or absurdity, that the world deals out.

The nightmare therefore distinguishes itself from dreams by having crossed a threshold. This threshold has to do with the understanding, acceptance, and integration of psychic contents. When that task is no longer possible, the psyche breaks off its natural activity; it pulls all the plugs, like the circuit breaker that saves a system from irreparable damage. This task, we have sensed, is exquisitely *human*. We are beginning to understand why, when experiments with animals show that we cannot demonstrate that they have nightmares.[6] Above all, we understand why infants, far more than adults, are "naturally" subject to nightmares.

The human being is the fruit of a long, extremely slow natural evolution. But the conditions in which we live grow ever more unnatural and are subject to accelerating cultural and technical mutations. Every newborn child is essentially identical to one from the Paleolithic era (if one can say that the point reached by human physical evolution after tens of millions of years has not substantially changed), while our cultural evolution is frenetic, constantly making leaps.

And so, of course, from its first day of life, a baby is immersed in an increasingly unnatural condition. For example, the overwhelmingly large numbers that are imposed on life repeatedly by an omnipotent human will do not belong to nature, and it is nature that has selected for the human puppy. Already in the mid-5th century B.C., Herodotus reported that those who witnessed the landing of numberless Persian troops in Greece believed they were confronted by a supernatural event.[7] Likewise, the nightmares of young children (or of those thrown into regression by profound stress—we shall take up an account of nightmares among the inmates of Auschwitz)—are often made of interminable and senseless repetitions of objects and persons: a palace with a thousand identical floors that the child must climb, or a train with a thousand coaches that it must count. However affectionate the family environment may be, and however attentive a family is in giving the child more than mere time, the child of the 21st century has not evolved to live in the 21st century, in which during a single day one can receive more stimulation than one's ancestors received in a year. The child's sleep often veers off into nightmare. Nightmare is an escape into the pathology and repression made necessary by the devastating cultural storms that blow into the psyche. The animal-human adapts successfully by devising tortuous complexities that the animal-animal never had. The waking human being often runs away into sleep (depression), while the one who sleeps flees into waking again (nightmare).[8]

The nightmare does not submit to sleep again—that is, to reinvoking a self-referential condition, to metabolism and production in the internal psychic sense—because it is the expression of the violent separation between a subjective interior reality and the objective but unnatural conditions imposed by civilization. The nightmare contains an excess of meanings that the psyche cannot manage to *com*-prehend and a surplus of tasks that the psyche cannot carry out. Its pathology has nothing strictly to do with psychiatry, but constitutes a special "multidisciplinary pathology." Psychiatry comes up against difficulty in defining it. The nightmare is the fruit of the irremediable alterity of human existence compared with that of the animal, and the consequence of its daily, inevitable, aggressive unnaturalness and incessant competitiveness.

Etymology offers a way of reconstructing the collective imaginary—contents that though unconscious have not disappeared—that our language leaves unspoken. And so it is interesting to notice that, in the chief European languages, the roots of words that signify *dream* simply return to a physiological fact—hence, animal fact—whereas all those that refer to *nightmare* are mythical images of a hostile being. Nightmare is therefore part of a culture, with its tales and traditions.

The Italian *sogno* and the Spanish *sueño* come from the Latin *somnium*, which in turn derives from *somnius*, sleep. In the German *Traum* and the English *dream*, the most frequent (though debatable) reference is to an ancient form of the verb *trügen*, to deceive. The French *rêve*, instead, stems from the Latin *vagus*: dreams correspond only to the wandering of the mind.

The concept of nightmare, by contrast, summons up the situations and characters of mythology. The Italian *incubo* comes from the Latin *incumbere*, which means "to crush or overwhelm." Similar to this is the Spanish *pesadilla*, which again refers to something that weighs so much that it flattens the dreamer. What is all this about? The ancients knew very well. French has remained quite explicit: *cauche-mar* stems from the ancient *caucher*, to push down, and from the Dutch *mare*, a mythical fantasy tied to the nightmare. *Mare* often qualified as feminine (in the patriarchal tradition in which the masculine was reserved for positive values, with the result that anything unknown, suspect, or plainly negative was automatically feminine, as happened with the figure of the witch) and appears in different languages, at least in archaic expressions: Dutch *mare*, German *Mahr*, Polish *zmara*, Czech *mura*, English *mare* or *maere*, etc. Modern English has *nightmare* since the simple *mare* has come to mean a horse, often retaining negative connotations. The German *Alp-traum*—literally a dream of the Alps—refers in reality (along with the more explicit *Alp-druck*, the crushing pressure of an alp) to a dangerous magical entity, *Alp* or *Alb*, related to the English "elf" (from which our Italian *elfo*), which the church (with its suspicion of traditional beliefs and its tendency to construct, in line with its God, a "monotheism of evil") simplified and equated with the devil.

Behind these remnants of imagery is a single pre-scientific explanation of the nightmare: a kind of sorceress brings it on, an invincible being, stronger than any dreamer, who smothers her victim. This image symbolically recapitulates the establishment of the ego, the product of rationality, which cannot manage to be stronger than the unconscious; and it declares that the male, an administrator of society, must recognize a greater feminine power that governs the psyche. (In passing, we might observe that the myths from which the idea of the nightmare originated remain silent about the fact that the nightmare certainly played a role, hardly a marginal one, in the persecution of witches.)

The contrast between the expectations created by mass-media simplification (for instance the kitschy Mulino Bianco brand in Italian advertising) and the sea of anxiety in which we are immersed today is particularly strong in infancy, unequipped by nature for meeting that "external nightmare" which is our world. The nightmares of the child are therefore manifestations of a deeply felt exercise in adaptation.

In general, individual evolution tends to repeat that of the species (ontogeny recapitulates phylogeny). Yet here this principle seems to be reversed. With its imperative "progress," the human realm shows itself to be ever more unnatural, the maker of nightmares, whereas the individual growing child frees itself from its own nightmares (its own inner devils) because it makes a pact with the outer devil: it exchanges its own individual pathology for that of the civilization that encircles it, slowly ingesting it.

In dreams, images combine and muddle themselves, seeking to produce a meaning and offering an outlet to diurnal psychic efforts as well as physical ones. But the dream degenerates into nightmare when it encounters a mortal adversary, or simply an intolerable one, or one that it simply cannot integrate.

One of the defining criteria that distinguish humans from animals—and which is acknowledged many times over—is the fact that murder is intraspecific to humans.[9] Psychoanalysis has said that the human being intuits what death is but somehow does not believe in its own death. It seeks to push death over onto someone else and at the same time eliminate him. The human being thereby kills two birds with one stone, removing not only his potential rival, but also his own death. Every animal has innate inhibitions that curb its aggression against members of its own species.[10] But when this intraspecificity (of the same species) becomes the other (another individual), these inhibitions begin to dissolve; then difference prevails over uniformity. A new being is born in whom psyche and culture depend on more than physical nature. Whereas the body, as we said, remains Paleolithic, dress and individual differences become infinite. Nothing any longer seems to be itself.

The animal perceives its surroundings with its eyes and nose, and so on. In the new being, what the senses perceive is already organized in, and subordinated to, mental images. From the moment that the notion of otherness breaks in on the mind, the fact that the environment is sensed as alien trumps sensing it as having to do with the same species. Ethology calls this process *cultural pseudo-speciation*[11]: the difference of the other—which in reality is cultural and relative—comes to be sensed as absolute, as if pertaining to another species of life. And if it belongs to another species, inhibitions fall away and killing becomes a natural matter.

If humankind is the only species whose members kill each other wholesale, this event, literally tragic, must have had a beginning. Our hypothesis lets us suppose that this route—its end point issuing in total war and genocide—must have been taken quite suddenly: as soon as You and I parted ways. Pseudo-speciation is a cultural mistake that takes itself as biological, scientific truth.[12] Racism tends to reproduce itself because it is born out of perceptions of difference that are multiplied by culture (the various codes of manners and dress, for example), but it was particularly devastating in the 19th century and the first half of the 20th, when it stepped out as science.

Establishing the other as different from me makes each of us a potential rival. If we, like the writers noted earlier, believe that this perception is stronger than any produced by consciousness, we must also acknowledge that the origin of consciousness is tragic and harrowing. It is likely that in so-called Western civilization there is no kind of knowledge that is older, and no literary genre more profound, than tragedy. From this perspective, the origin of consciousness has its seat in a traumatic, nearly intolerable event.

Its consequences are double. In the outer world, one moves from an unconscious coexistence, the fusion path of the herd animal, to a network of conscious relationships, whose new element is mistrust, hostility, and, in limit situations, the need to eliminate the other guy. We have hypothesized that the beginning of this unnatural activity—the murder of our own kind—coincides with a psychic innovation: awareness that the other person is irremediably different. Both developments are tragic and irrevocable.

In the inner world, when the psyche begins to perceive an ineradicable difference, it too begins to have not simply dreams but nightmares.

The nightmare is in fact the corresponding partner, on the inner plane, to a homicidal attack. The parallel is doubly powerful. The pure nightmare, out of which one startles awake, describes an encounter with a mortal enemy—not only from a dark physical sensation like that of a mortal wound, but also from awareness, tragic to the point of being intolerable, that the other person is overwhelmingly alien. Therefore, everyone who faces off against another person in a nightmare is a potential killer. It does not matter if in the nightmare I annihilate or am annihilated, or if the dream figures are human beings or horrifying anomalies, because in either case *the protagonist of the nightmare is a radically annihilating emotion, and therefore a killer.* But in a way even more profound, the nightmare inwardly matches up with the new situation of otherness outside. Just as externally one no longer lives the herd life of unconsciousness, but begins to meet others and sense their difference as intolerable, so the dream is no longer largely made up of partly distinct presences (so much so that psychoanalysis reads them as "inner characters"), but places at the center of the action an "other" so different that the dream is no longer able to carry on a dialogue with the dreamer's ego, and simply short-circuits the psyche awake—as if to say, "Look out, off-limits to the ego! Here comes someone you cannot metabolize!"

With the nightmare, the so-called unconscious has to some extent run up against the personality that has been rejected. It would correspond to the image of a villain or monster, which the dreamer on waking will strongly resist accepting as part of his personality. (The fact that, after a nightmare, it is difficult to go back to sleep suitably manifests the refusal to return to *my* oneiric world, since an assassin lives there.) This "inner character," this unexpected and dreadful part of the dreamer's personality, is the right expression, in dream symbols, of the new and terrible quality that separates the human from the animal: the destroyer and killer.

It is not nice to think about, but it is true to life. Before there was Christian *agapé*, long indeed before ethnic, national, or social solidarity, the foundational quality for the development of human consciousness was destructiveness. As we have said, archaeology, paleontology, and anthropology, as Eibl-Eibesfeldt has summarized them,[13] testify that no matter how far back in time one goes, one finds men killing other men.

Humanity in its natural state is not something such as Rousseau proposed, decked out a little with the Enlightenment and Romanticism, but an experiment far more complicated than the one described by Anthony Pagden.[14] As Freud has said, the natural human being must necessarily be repressed. In every place and time, as Jacobucci says in his fine book on intolerance, rejection of the other tends to trump acceptance.[15] Therefore, as Umberto Eco reiterates in keeping faith with Freud's pessimism, "intolerance, like violence, is not an illness but a disposition quite natural for the human animal."[16]

"Take No Prisoners"

On July 22, 1900, the German Kaiser, addressing an expeditionary force about to leave for China, without realizing it uttered the manifesto of the century: "When the enemy comes before you he must be destroyed. Offer no conditions. Take no prisoners (*Gefangene* [*werden*] *nicht gemacht*)."[17]

The 20th century is the century of massacres, ethnic cleansing, genocide. The century of death was kicked off with these words in a country that would prove to be particularly fertile territory for the harvests of evil.[18] One of the most brutal and sadistic of colonial enterprises was launched, a qualitative leap down the long road of refusing the other. Europeans had no miserable African tribes before them, but the world's oldest civilization and its treasures. In ruining it, to the simple contempt with which they had annihilated the Africans they added a secret envy. They could not stop at simply killing the Chinese; they needed also to paint the killing fields with cultural, religious, and ideological justifications.

For the first time, Japan had the honor of dividing the colonial spoils with the West. As is well known, Japanese modernization was based on reproducing Western technology down to the last detail. Thus, in the 1930s, they carried out the conquest of China all by themselves, by applying and perfecting these methods; but the West—perhaps because of new envy, perhaps because they were repressing their bad conscience—defined them as war criminals.

The psychology corresponding to these historical events—in particular the matter of taking no prisoners—inheres in the radical rejection of the other that we have discussed from the outset.

Already during World War I, the problem of dealing with the other had become explosive. On both sides, the refusal to take prisoners grew. In the uninterrupted bestiality of combat and the unprecedented scope of propaganda promoting hatred of the enemy, this problem felt so alien to us that we could not assimilate it, even when the other took the form of a herd penned in by barbed wire in a concentration camp.[19] The relentless hammering by propaganda that pictures the enemy as subhuman, perverse, and infidel instills in soldiers an absolute need to annihilate him. Thus, a world in which the adversary must still have a place becomes unimaginable: even when imprisoned, proclaim the insinuations of propaganda, your adversary will still try to stab you in the back.

In the bloody swirl of fighting, whoever throws down his weapons and raises his hands is shot with sadistic relish by the one who has kept his gun in hand. Should an entire unit survive to this fateful moment and surrender, the officers in charge assign some soldiers to conduct them to a camp in the rear. When giving the order, they also tip the wink: waste no time over these subhumans who, as we know, kill our troops when they take them prisoner. When the escorts return to the front, they report to the same officers that their prisoners tried to revolt and had to be shot. The officers congratulate them and ask no further questions.

The fact that senior officers also approved such behavior makes it clear that more than psychopathology was involved. It confirms that at the front a mass psychosis was at work. Beyond being among the gravest violations of international law, in the end this behavior also compromised the military advantages of all parties. As the Scottish historian Niall Ferguson has shown, trench warfare tended to prolong itself endlessly. The daily slaughter notwithstanding, whether among the Central Powers or the Allies, new levies of troops were thrown in each year to replace those lost. In spite of the introduction of new weapons systems, the stability of trench warfare stymied attempts to bleed the enemy by increasing the kill ratio. In this stalemate, the factor decisive for victory was the encouragement of desertion and surrender by the enemy, and so shooting whoever gave himself up as a prisoner instead produced exactly the contrary effect.[20]

In the collective madness, however, simply the appearance of the enemy (not of his weapons, since we are speaking of disarmed combatants) produced a short circuit in the collective mind. That mind, through a mechanism quite similar to that of the nightmare, reacted irrationally, with totalizing rejection. Just as the nightmare escapes the encounter with something too alien, destroying the dream and returning to familiar waking life, the soldiers, by destroying their disarmed enemies, escape the encounter with an adversary too novel and too strange, taking flight into a reality that they know, namely, by going back to killing.

It is no accident, then, that precisely during the Great War the problem of "shell shock" exploded uncontrollably, with soldiers suffering nightmares and constant restlessness. In fact, the nightmare is the inner correlative of the daily encounter between enemies in a total war, of which the Great War was the first unqualified example. The nightmare is also the total rejection of the adversary. In what we call a dream, the psyche elaborates on the encounter of ego with other. When the dream transforms itself into nightmare, the ego enters a state of shock and calls off as impossible any dialogue or integration. In full flight from the encounter, it wakes up.

The refusal to deal with prisoners is therefore not reducible to a simple problem of military logistics in time of war. It is also the symbolic expression of an *allophobia*, an indiscriminate and totalizing fear of others, which invades the 20th century as a mass psychosis. In this psychological incapacity, which war translates into quotidian inhumanity, the history of World War I has assigned to Italy a wretched pre-eminence. Italy alone refused, in the end, to have anything to do with its own troops once they had been taken prisoner. In contrast to all other nations in that war, it declined, contravening the Red Cross, to give them either clothing or rations through Red Cross intermediation. According to the reconstruction by historian Angelo Del Boca, this fact alone brought death to some 100,000 of the 600,000 Italian soldiers taken prisoner by the Austrians.[21] The rationale for this brutality was simply that they should never have surrendered. In this respect, Italy anticipated Stalin's treatment of Russian soldiers liberated from the Germans at the end of the World War II, whom he sent to the Gulag or exterminated in other ways. Surrender was equated with desertion.

Naturally, the explosive increase in nightmares and anxiety conditions brings in its wake a new, important discipline: military psychiatry.

Already during the American Civil War, the first military hospital for mental cases had appeared. But after the war, it was shut down.

The shocks that incapacitated soldiers were, for the first time, considered as an illness (in contrast to dereliction of duty) by the Russians in their war against Japan in 1905. Silently they struck a horrible sort of deal: military psychiatry obtained the ideological advantage of denying that soldiers in possession of their sanity could refuse to kill; and soldiers were granted the favor of allowing themselves some authorized rest.

Gradually, military psychiatry slid downhill toward anti-psychiatric principles: to philopathological ones, if one may say so. With World War I, the prevailing doctrine came by way of the American Armed Forces from Dr. Thomas Salmon, later elected president of the American Psychiatric Association. Every combat unit was assigned military psychiatrists, who at the first sign of panic or nightmares among troops moved them immediately to the rear, giving them light therapy and rest for a few days, before sending them back into the line.[22] This "therapy" carried to extremes the model of the first Russian interventions, obtaining a maximum percentage of recoveries because it alleviated symptoms without letting anyone (who could still walk) escape returning to the front, and without rehabituating them to the idea that there exists a world free of enemies or daily massacre. It improved the efficiency of weaker individuals—or simply more sensitive ones—at the cost of pretending that the front was not the cause of the pathology, and therefore that it could be a destination of recovery.

If, after wiping out the enemy militarily, the fighting man has also erased the psychological existence of the other, he still finds himself confronting the landscape of war. Here, too, World War I created new conditions that favored the development of allophobia: the hammering of artillery, the first aerial bombardments, and flamethrowers nourished the temptation to do away with the landscape itself. This illusion grew into the intoxication of omnipotence, particularly among the American armed forces, who ended up developing defoliants and atomic weapons.

We can now return to our consideration that war in the 20th century has violently multiplied the power to kill, not only through its titanic technological capacity, but also through the propaganda of hate and its psychopathic consequences for the masses. So, one may speak of total war not only because it has involved the entire industrial apparatus of modernity, but also because it has involved the whole psychological superstructure (collective consciousness, through mass media). Participants are kept in complete and continuous mobilization, pressed upon like ancient warriors hounded by the Furies.[23] War and the hate machine simplify things, permitting regression, the abdication of individual responsibility to the herd.

In modern terms, these conditions should be described as mass borderline states, if psychiatry (not only the military kind) were to take care, as it should, of mass mental disturbances that are not simply the aggregate of individual ones. When this total mobilization is introjected, as usually happens with more sensitive people, it takes over the whole person, day and night. Nightmares invade the mind. Coming awake, the dreamer finds himself in a state of vigilance that blocks his return to sleep and sustains, whether as a memory of the nightmare or as anxiety, what plagues him while awake. He has the worst of both worlds.

Foremost in this general desolation, a specific desolation of our own comes with observing the role of psychiatry. It could use its tools to diagnose homicidal fury as the source of this devastation, but frequently it has been "patriotic," an attitude that leads to patching the victims back together so that they can be sent back into the line, to be torn to pieces in body and mind.[24]

World War I, concentrating millions of soldiers for several years in the claustrophobic situation of the trenches, also produced a concentration of nightmares. In the wars that have followed, however, the front line has hardly remained stationary. The front has been radically dispersed, and with it the experience of combat. Consequently, both nightmares, and psychopathology more generally, have been systematically dislocated. With every new war a new pathology has come along, in the classifications of American military psychiatry, as if diagnosed for the first time.[25] The virtual eradication of conventional front lines has contributed to making war a total affair from the demographic point of view as well: in every conflict that takes place now, the number of civilians killed exceeds that of those killed in combat. And the demographics of nightmare follow suit. Confronted with military conduct that intentionally includes terrorism,[26] ethnic cleansing, and genocide, distinctions between military and civilian psychiatry simply crumble. Nightmares of the wildest variety appear among the most diverse groups of people.

I shall close by recalling the story of a patient that inspires hope and despair at the same time.

Martin was a poor adolescent, an orphan who in his own country was discriminated against for being German. To redeem these three factors, he voluntarily enlisted in the Wehrmacht at the beginning of World War II, lying about his age. After a brief period of training he was transferred to the Eastern Front, where the greatest attack of all time was being mounted. As we now also know from historical research, the orders given to officers at the outset of Operation Babarossa were quite different from those on the Western Front. France had been conquered, but also preserved as a possible ally, whereas the Soviet Union was going to be crushed and turned into territory for colonization.

Something changed inside Martin—spontaneously and irrevocably—when he heard his commanding officer exhort the unit: "In this war we are taking no prisoners." The adolescent became a man. Martin, however, did not realize that immediately. He knew only that he was upset, psychically disturbed. Every night brought him nightmares, more or less the same.

They featured an anonymous, indistinct throng, brought together for some unknown reason, bound for some unknown destination. Into this grey, meaningless, absurd mass of people breaks a group of soldiers. They begin selecting people based on absurd and irrelevant details: those with white trousers go to one side and are saved, while those with dark ones go to the other and are shot. Always, and only at the last instant, Martin realizes that he is among the survivors. But anxiety wakes him all the same, and for a long time he cannot get back to sleep.

As we know from the histories, in this phase the Wehrmacht's advance was swift. The Red Army restricted itself to retreating, leaving scorched earth behind; for a long time Martin's unit did not fire a shot. But one morning there happened what sooner or later happens in every war. They were told to move carefully, weapons at the ready. Shots, then orders to hit the dirt and commence firing! A group of Russian soldiers ran towards them, blazing away in turn. The confusion in Martin's brain reached its peak when, for the first time in his life, he leveled a gun at a man.

"Before pulling the trigger, before the burst of fire, I turned the gun on myself. Even now I can't explain why, but I know how I did it, I remember the act very well. I've never told anyone. I still feel ashamed. Today nothing seems sillier or more hateful than the Wehrmacht, and nothing more criminally stupid than the irresponsible enlistment I chose. I'm ashamed that I ever followed its discipline; but at the same time, however absurd it may be, I'm also ashamed that I disobeyed."[26]

In Martin's nightmares, three anonymous groups appear: the soldier killers and two groups of victims. This vague and anonymous condition is common in nightmares; according to Carole Beebe Tarantelli, the nightmares described by Primo Levi in *If This Is a Man* express the disintegration of the ego under the violence of the concentration camp.[27] In the majority of nightmares, the opposition is between two individuals or two groups. In order to represent a mortal danger, the nightmare generally shows an opposition that is absolute and, as such, also irresolvable. The only solution is flight from the situation in the dream, into waking. This also occurs in Martin's nightmares, but the triangular situation seems to offer a novelty and an alternative. The other singular thing about them is the fact that they seem to anticipate his traumatic armed encounter. How can this inversion of sequence be possible?

In reality, the trauma had already come to Martin when the officers had said that they could take no prisoners. What could that mean in a war that is called just? And what had it begun to say to his clear and artless conscience? The encounter with the enemy, which had not been the real trauma but its follow-on, was speedily final in its ripening, which came entirely within, unconscious, and enacted itself autonomously. At the instant he pulled the trigger, Martin had unconsciously reinterpreted his nightmare. As a nightmare typically does, the untenable confrontation with evil had decidedly forced an exit from the situation. But, purely from anxiety and in the disorientation of battle, much like the powerlessness and disorientation that vie with each other in the nightmare, a moral force—which the personality will reveal in due course—is set in train. The ego was not left hidden in the crowd, and had chosen which side it wished to be with. His nightmares had said that it was not enough to be among the victims who were saved. However, he was not capable (it was not a matter of choice) of siding with human beings who killed other human beings. Able to be only an absolute objector, he had to use any means at hand to oppose himself to the soldier who kills; and, in order to do that, he could only shoot himself. Evidently, this was the more acceptable price to pay.

The god, or destiny, that takes care of the courageous and the foolhardy alike, took care that none of his officers saw by whose gun Martin had been wounded. He was decorated for the reported wound and assigned to a long convalescence. In the event, the same god saved him from other battles and made him a prisoner of the Allies. Martin began to read avidly, to discuss philosophy and politics. The nightmares gradually abated.

After the war, he became somebody well known in his line of work and in the culture. Engaged in many causes, though not in active organizing, he was as unshakably reserved as he was pacifist. Although he warmed to respect, admiration, and affection, Martin nonetheless remained a tragic and tormented person, the victim of insomnia, migraines, and depressions.

One day, for the second time, he turned a weapon on himself.

He took his own life as a brother in secret to Primo Levi. Like him, he had struggled for decades to free himself from the nightmare, without completely succeeding. Martin felt, however, as with the historical nightmare of the war, that he was partly an accomplice. Yet the reflection of that in him, his personal nightmare, was not only negative. It had granted him a choice, at the cost of his hiding it from the world. He had finished with his assignment, a very particular form of heroism. Martin lived and acted only from within. And, twice only, unable to do otherwise, he took up arms against himself.

CHAPTER FIVE

Reductivism: Against Ismene

A ghost is haunting globalization. An evil that, little by little, can devour everything in its path, but that moves so quietly that it raises no alarm. This specter is not some kind of economic risk or mischance, which today's world is always in a position to overcome sooner or later. Material lack is not what haunts us now, but a cultural and spiritual impoverishment that can go on for centuries, becoming definitive for us.

Reductivism is poverty of thought, of total understanding, and of compassion. Reductivism is not the extreme poverty described by economics, for economics, like science generally, builds on its findings and follows a step-by-step progression. No, it is a wretchedness of the soul. And in order to deal with psychic scarcities and indigence, every single person must start over again from scratch. The task is a global affair, a responsibility held at large, which each and every inheritor, each son or daughter of the situation, will have to hoist on his or her back and carry alone.

The culture of the era reflects itself in each of us. If that culture is unrefined and brutish, impoverishing our humanity, the individual finds himself inhabiting a tragic tension. Every society lays down a code of norms, usually unwritten, to which we must pay attention because the majority demands it. On the other hand, in order to avoid spiritual impoverishment, the individual for whom complaining is not enough must step out and take the lead, being the first to make corrective experiments. This tragic dilemma is our own condition today. The malady called "reductivism," the impoverishment of spirit and soul, appears to be an epoch-making tendency of Western society that, during the period of globalization, is becoming the civilization imposed on everyone.

One telling critique of contemporary reductivism turns up in the acceptance speech by Ricardo Lagos Escobar, the former president of Chile, on the occasion of his receiving an honorary degree from the University of Salamanca.[1] According to Lagos, after the fall of the Berlin Wall we have been treated to three kinds of reductivism, three contractions in our conduct of public affairs (letting us speak of new forms of political and social philosophy).

First among these three, *democracy is gradually being reduced to governability*, that is, to its more functional aspect, immediate and normative or regulatory—though to the detriment of any more profound conceptions. These latter conceptions usually link up with either foundational ideals (expressed in various national constitutions) or in projects to be carried out through time. (We will remark further on the manner in which reductivism assaults continuity through time.)

As for the second major contraction, *economic freedom has become reduced, increasingly, to the freedom of the market, to the free movement of prices*, while for millions of people the first economic freedom remains that of the ability to find enough food. Only once freed from elemental need can people make use of their secondary liberty, to enter economic markets and devote themselves to gainful activities of their own choosing.

Finally, according to Lagos, after September 11, 2001 *international politics has restricted itself to the struggle against terrorism.* And with respect to the developed world, permit me to add, *also to the control of immigration.* In only a few years, in fact, in countries such as France or Italy, immigration has become the very core of politics, at least for those popular movements that stir up primitive emotions and momentary consensus. As a result, instead of helping those who fight against the backwardness that sustains immigration, we strengthen the defenses that keep immigrants far away—that is, we harden the wealth differential, precisely that separation of rich from poor that causes migrations. In fact, outlays for international aid remain substantially the same, while funds for immigration control in the USA have quintupled during the last twenty years, tripled in Germany over the last ten, and doubled in Great Britain in the last three.[2]

In other words, global expansion makes the continents the common possession of all humanity, whereas we, out of fear and paranoia, seek to reduce and constrict the world. Only rarely is the rediscovery of the local a positive thing rather than a new defensiveness.

Numbers are always ruthless. There seems to be no better way of describing how the West is reducing what the Christian tradition called the neighbor to the stranger, and then, ever so gradually, to the enemy. We always believe that we ourselves are a bit more civilized than our predecessors, and sometimes that is true. But the facts now before us bespeak a gradual drying up of the wellsprings of feeling, tragically similar to that which Hazel Rosenstrauch has summarized in her 1988 book, *How Neighbors Became Jews*, and Ulrich Beck in his 1995 volume, *How Neighbors Were Turned into Jews.* Both studies analyze how the reduction of the neighbor to the foreign and the odious led to the West's most notorious crimes against humanity.

When speaking of modern reductivism, therefore, we are also referring to the creation of a moral desert. Aridity does not advance across the Sahara unaided. Forms of reductivism that look quite dissimilar have in common the loss of both intelligence and courage. We need to fight desertification not just in the outer world but in the inner world as well.

The Concept

To discuss reductivism, we must first of all define and lay out our terms. By reductivism we mean a cognitive attitude that replaces many kinds of experience and points of view with one alone. Such an attitude seduces the observer with its functionality, but impoverishes the object that is being observed. It prefers technical and scientific forms of explanation, but to the detriment of both understanding and the depth of experience. Its cousin in a pragmatic vein is specialization.

There also exists, rather forgotten, a kind of reductivism that affords strength and concentration. We could call it a "reduction to the heart," a stripping down to core principles. This attitude dispenses with unimportant particulars. From the parts it turns to the whole. From the superfluous it turns toward the original inspiration.

The Renaissance affirmed this positive version of reduction. According to Machiavelli, in difficult times a society renews itself, and assures its endurance, by reducing its powers to those that served as its original inspiration. "Speaking of republics," he writes, "this reduction to principle comes about either by external accident or through intrinsic prudence."[3] Italy undergoes rebirth or "renaissance" by turning to the most important values of classical antiquity, precisely as the Church did, which already would have gone terminally soft before the Reformation had it not been shaken up by personalities such as St. Francis of Assisi, who called for liberation from elaborate involvements in politics and material life through a return to pure origins.

Machiavelli spoke not simply as a Florentine of the Renaissance, but also as a universal genius for all time. Of the three great creative eras of the West—the Renaissance, the Enlightenment, and Romanticism—two based themselves on this return to essence: the first in a rebirth of classical values, the third in a spirit that it attributed to Rome.

Nevertheless, today when one speaks of reductivism one is referring not to a tendency from the center or heart but to a "rational" one.

It is no accident that this tendency has developed from within Western thinking itself. It is a constant of Western history that a governing power regulates the mental processes inside people as well as regulating the world around them. Mystery is replaced by clarity, and confusion by rationality. There is no gainsaying the advantages of this functionalism, which already stands out among the merits of early Greek thinking. In this sense, the early Eleatic philosophers are precocious secularists and naturalists, beginning with Democritus.

Philosophy fosters science, and that sponsorship then promotes the reduction of inquiry from the supernatural to the natural, and from the multiform and fluid to the uniform and rigid, from the magical to the causal. The most significant shift of this kind was achieved by Descartes. In his *Rules for the Direction of the Mind* (1628, published in 1701), it is "reduction" that figures as the fifth practical rule for the discovery of natural truths. The Cartesian formula "I think, therefore I am" (*cogito ergo sum*) reduces psychic life to the conscious ego. By the time Nietzsche wrote in 1886 that, in contrast to the I, "It thinks" (*Es denkt*), and when Freud in 1926 declared that "[t]here was something in me that was … stronger than I was" (*Es war etwas in mir, was … stärker war als ich*), the restricted, reductive conception of the psyche had already been widespread for centuries.

Something very like this, at bottom, also happens in theology.

Carried beyond the Roman Empire, the West leaves the shores of polytheism and finds harbor in monotheism (in the form of a sectarian Judaism called Christianity). The gods—theological agencies or "causes"—are reduced from an infinite number to a single one. The mysteries, too, which at first were numberless, survive only in a few dogmas. The powers and aims of divinity become more comprehensible. Christian precepts reduce everything to love, along with purposes and motives—particularly in politics, which become more pleasant and more rational. Coming down through the centuries to the era of secularism, this tendency applies the same optimistic outlook to history as well. When they finally add it all up, however, and notice that Christians, Enlightenment types, the various progressivists, and the modernizers are all busy killing each other off, it is a bit too late to turn things around.

Values and Time

For the sake of brevity, I will unify the reductivist cavalcade of our Western world under two headings: *the reduction of values* and *the reduction of time.*

On several occasions, I have discussed the loss of the unity left to us by the classical world, and the consequences of that loss for the world in which we find ourselves living now.[4] Greek tragedy was for everyone and for all time. It was understood by the intellectuals and the least literate of Athenians alike. It was packed with dramatic pleasure as well as with moral teaching for future generations. It was a religious ritual (one honoring Dionysus; it was no Broadway pastime as nowadays!) and counsel for everyday living.

Just as no lay morality existed separately from a religious one, so also no art stood on its own, funded by a "department of the beautiful." Art was part of the cult offered to the gods or to society in its affiliation with divinity (Athens derived its name directly from the goddess Athene).

Virtue was unitary, both ethical and aesthetic. Not by chance, the idea of beauty and the idea of justice came to convergence in a single concept, of *kalós kai agathós*, or the-beautiful-and-the-good, out of which Greek formed the noun *kalokagathía*, a virtue that is at one and the same time beauty and justice. It taught the Greeks to respect this pairing just as the Hebrew commandment teaches an identical respect for one's mother and father: as if they are one and the same. An ethical offense and an offense against good taste came down to the same thing. The elegance of a temple dedicated to one of the gods and inspiration for the conduct of life that came from cult worship of the god were, at root, the same thing.

Christianity began to separate these two virtues, rationalizing morality and also placing it on a higher plane. Nonetheless, as already noted, the practice of Christian life until the time of the Reformation preserved many aspects of the classical world.

Monotheistic asceticism did not supplant classical values. Over the centuries, there came about a compromise with them. The saints represent many of the same types of character as the gods to those who turn to them in prayer, a practice that cultivates that same individual quality in a way not very different from what occurred in Greco-Roman polytheism.

Before the modern era, religious life was a total experience, whether in the communal sense or because it was integrally ethical and aesthetic. The religious ceremony of the Renaissance, not unlike a typical ritual in classical antiquity, is an immersion in a myth to which one cannot fail to lend credence, through either the elevation of its message or the beauty that communicates it, both being essential. Once again, therefore, it is governed by unitary or integrative virtue (*kalokagathía*). In an epoch that lacked communications media, communal sharing took place through public ceremonies. Those who could not read took part, at no expense, in civic and religious rituals—graced by musical accompaniment, painting, costume, and processional regalia—that afforded experiences of beauty that remain among the finest of all time.

In my recent Fay Lectures on *Ethics and Analysis*, I have developed one hypothesis about the relationships between ethics and aesthetics.[5] In building a truly moral society, the respect for justice and the good must not be separated from respect for the beautiful. In classical Athens or in Renaissance Florence the "quality of life" was high not only because it was constantly nourished by beauty, but also because such societies, as well as being large and complex for their times, afforded places for harmonious conviviality that were not plagued by crime. A person could enjoy the emotion of being fully satisfied without becoming obsessive. In harmony with that kind of aesthetics, the ethical experience repaid itself in the same way. On ritual occasions it promoted social behaviors as being more than abstract rules, by melting or fusing the beautiful-and-good, and thereby nourished a sense of belonging to a unified and ideal community.[6]

The poles between which this harmonious society formed itself can be summarized in two ideas from Machiavelli: the Piazza or public square where the masses congregate, and the Palazzo or palace in which the power-elite could seclude themselves. In Florence and above all in Athens (to oversimplify, of necessity), the public square is still an area that is communal in every sense, in which the values of justice come to be decided and the artistic laboratory carries out its experiments.

Inexorably, through the centuries, beauty was lured away from the public square and sequestered in the palace. This is a highly visible aspect of the reductivism that we are discussing here. The shared life of the Renaissance *Comune* gave way to the *Signoria*. With time, even the dukes who promoted the arts through patronage, such as the Medici, dragged music and painting into the confines of their private chambers. Art, once the essential handmaiden of ritual and public expression, became, as Walter Benjamin has observed, a secular object of private ownership, a collector's item. In the end, art is reduced to an investment.

One of Leonardo's Madonnas today can fetch a million dollars. And yet the better part of its value has been lost down the centuries, because value itself has devolved to *economic value*, to market price. All that we feel from the original radiance of art is an invisible shadow cast by the commotion that lit the fire.[7] Once upon a time, art acted; it was the subject. It has been reduced now to an object, a passive thing, inert upon the wall. In spirit, the community bows down in grief. In order to endure the conflict, we have invented museums, and we carry the mummy inside.

Much the same thing has happened to a non-material treasure, the act of reading and listening. Before printing multiplied books, reading remained tied to oral culture. With only a few texts available, reading was a public affair, carried on out loud. But one day, in Milan, Augustine stood transfixed by what he saw. Bishop Ambrose was reading from a book at top speed without making a sound, barely moving his eyes and lips.[8] Two great figures in Christianity meet at that moment, but two human needs divorce themselves forever: functionalism triumphs over companionable ritual and also over the aesthetic experience that goes with it. From then on, reading is much more practical and greatly speeds up; the destiny of oral reading stands marked as that of a loser—just as does that of the handwritten letter with the coming of e-mail. Reading as an experience of the sacred text withdraws from the public square and *reduces itself,* enclosing itself within the walls of a new, metaphorical "palace," the individual personality.

Then, little by little, the two poles of society altogether contract themselves into one, the palace.

In a parallel fashion, values gradually strip themselves of their aesthetic quality, reducing themselves to ethics. The idea of wholeness or totality dispenses with flesh and blood: what remains is the skeleton of the moral law. And then ethics wither in turn, reducing themselves to norms, regulations that invade every field. Instead of aesthetic value, originally shared by everyone, there is nothing more than the necessary and the functional. It is impossible to justify the suffering of this kind of reductivist acceleration, this aesthetic and ethical devolutionary speedup, for it is in no one's interest to endure its impact.

Such aesthetic anorexia is all one with the materialistic and commercial reduction of values that Max Weber characterized as a *disenchantment of the world.*

Functionalism strips human flesh from bone wherever people cannot perform like machines or where they are not strictly necessary in administrative terms. In passing from a medieval to a modern basis, and thereby becoming far more active and complicated, society demands an increasing number of norms, simply in order to function, to govern a growing population that moves into new forms of activity and a proliferating web of commerce. National politics in most countries reduces itself to rituals that serve efficiency—secularism in operation—and international politics reduces ancient civilizations to mere resource reservoirs exploited by European and American colonialism.

This reductive conversion of entire other worlds into functional appendages of the developed West leaves behind a twisted sense of guilt. To deal with this appalling outcome, we have invented anthropology, the science that Octavio Paz has called "the remorse of the Occident." The new graveyard that serves as the repository for this conflict will be known as the Museum of Ethnology, standing alongside the one dedicated to art.

Myth feeds the very sense of being alive. Science, which reduces life to a mummy, nourishes only those explanations spawned by reason. People who possess myths also live full lives. But those who are fed a steady diet of scientific demonstrations can fall into depression, even suicide.

How were all of the world's integral or holistic values animated by a magical spell? It was through the traditional tale or story, the bones inside the shimmering muscles of an artistically rendered myth. Theater enacted inside temple or church, the musical cycle, the painted array of frescoes were sacred story, something the public shared in common, whose beauty moved people from within (*com*-motion).

The book, originally public and sacred, has become today a private commodity; and theater has devolved from total ritual into *entertainment*. Everything has made its definitive exit from the public square, to hide itself away in numberless palace-apartments, sovereign one-room flats, where anxiety and solitude reign.

But the reduction of storytelling—in which meaning goes on a quest—to a mere amusement is also the loss of that perspective which brings human beings into solidarity and leads them to build a society. We sorrow together over how humankind has had to lose its integral values, how immorality has undergone standardization, and how each succeeding decade brings forth new outrages. But what models can humanity turn to any more? The unity of ethics and aesthetics has been dissolved by time; beauty has been barricaded within museums; and story as the best-seller or the tabloid (and television) has subjected the masses to aesthetic abuse. Under this onslaught, people assume the posture of passivity rather than participation, and voyeurism instead of passion. Storytelling, turned commercial and banal and anesthetized, has been reduced to pornography, indifferently sexual or violent. Analogously, the ideals made glamorous through media exposure make up well-defined status levels of *wealth porn*. (By "pornography," I mean a reduction to the kind of pleasure that is sought in private and for a brief period of time.) Psychopathology tells us that victims of abuse tend to repeat or reconstitute the situation in which they were abused. If the medium is already its own message (and therefore has no purpose), the mass of people, *ab*-used by continuous messages, remains imprisoned within them, and like the medium this mass functions without purpose or aim. And people feel themselves alive only by remaining victims of abuse.

In contrast to what happened with the naked body presented by Michelangelo or the violence recounted by Homer, numerous studies show that today a strict correspondence holds between the quantity of violent shows or scenes consumed in mass culture and the frequency of violent acts and sexual assaults. In the process, both love and war, the full-bodied conditions of passion and combat, become uprooted from their texts—the integral story or tale—and are reduced to items for sale.

If storytelling has withered in this way, something similar has happened to the members of its audience, or rather its spectators. One anxiety reaction to the globalization that has done away with limits and borders everywhere has been an extreme reinforcement of the value of one's own four walls. The turning point comes in the American suburbs of the 1970s and 1980s, when it became "obligatory" to give children their own rooms.[9] And also a personal stereo, a personal TV, a personal computer. All of which leave one isolated in space.

But Western modernization also strands one in time—and cuts one off from time—in a pointillistic and lonely present. By thus closing off the present, one erases the temporal horizons of past and future.

Dante's treatise on politics exhorts us to continue admiring the exemplars of our past and, at the same time, to practice modesty. The true human being does not labor for the present moment, but in order to become part of the past.

> All those who incline toward the love of truth because a higher nature leads them to, observe one thing above all; they work for those who will come after them, so that their inheritors can use the fruits of their labors, just as they themselves have been served by the labors of those who went before them.[10]

The modern West, on the contrary, ideologically has come to justify the eradication of the past. Let us call to mind two famous manifestos. John O'Sullivan's article "The Great Nation of Futurity," published in 1839,[11] known to the wider public as the manifesto of *Manifest Destiny* (the play on words is not incidental), among other things proclaimed:

> Our national birth was the beginning of a new history.... We may confidently assume that our country is destined to be the great nation of futurity....
>
> What friend of human liberty, civilization and refinement, can cast his view over the past history of monarchies and

> aristocracies of antiquity, and not deplore that they ever existed? . . . We have no interest in the scenes of antiquity, only as lessons of avoidance of nearly all examples.

On February 20, 1909, Filippo Tommaso Marinetti published in *Le Figaro* his "Manifesto of Futurism," which says, among other things:

> There is no greater beauty than that of battle. A work of art which lacks the aggressive thrust can never be a masterpiece . . . .
>
> We mean to glorify war—the only health the world knows—militarism, patriotism, the act of destruction.
>
> We shall smash the museums, the libraries, schools of every kind . . . .

These two manifestos have overturned Dante's perspective. The past becomes a heap of ruins that teaches one never to look back. The reduction of time to a present turned exclusively towards the future comes about through an intentional and ideological destruction of exemplary models, whether ethical or aesthetic, from the past.

Our model ancestors are in fact quite diverse. In order to crush them, these two manifestos begin by invoking ideology *to reduce human beings from the past to persons who do not matter.* And in so doing, they mean to reject diversity and to settle its hash for all time.

The first such ideology flows out of ethnocentrism into Social Darwinism, on into racism, and into the oppression or extermination of native peoples. It is also fed by a mistaken American exceptionalism, according to which the USA is exempt from any connections to the past and can therefore ignore them in enterprises of the moment (for example, considering the reasons why the British failed in their adventure in Iraq in the '20s as irrelevant when making the decision to do the very same thing eight decades later).

The second ideology, which brought shame to my own country, received its baptism from the two World Wars, the several fascisms, and their genocidal racism. When one begins climbing down the stairway of discrimination—as Primo Levi has put it—one does well to remember that at the end stands Auschwitz. The humiliation or degradation of the past is a discrimination against time, and finds its arrogant partner in the political humiliation of other nations and races.

To be sure, too much of the past can be lethal in the present: once again, Primo Levi's life testifies to that fact. But the negation of the past also kills. Psychiatrists in Argentina know this all too well, having discovered the "Malvine Syndrome" (in connection with the Falkland Islands War). The Argentine soldiers were seduced into fighting against Britain with promises of military glory. With the collapse of the Galtieri dictatorship and all its rhetoric, the only result was the shamed silence of an entire society. After more than two decades, the one major historical consequence is the alarming rise in the suicide rate among veterans: more soldiers have died at their own hand than lost their lives in the war itself.

The fear of diversity, therefore, is also the fear of time, because time creates differences. I am afraid of diversity because I am ignorant, but I am afraid of the future as well, because I don't know how I will change. This reduction of time to the present, that present from which Horace and Lorenzo the Magnificent produced the beautiful,[12] changes into its negative twin through the Western phenomenon known as consumerism.

We acquire every kind of object, and we must get all of it right away, without really needing it, because we believe neither in our own happiness nor in our future. As for that, we swallow more than we can use. A chocolate bar pleases me, but no sooner do I lay my hands on it than I gobble it down whole, in a flash. As with the future, so with respect for limits: they have been entirely lost in our education.

I would like to swallow up everything that I want to have, but that act—like the horizon, which moves ahead of us as we advance—diminishes by that much how much we can eat. We now consume the future, as we do with our resources and the environment, just as Chronos devoured the flesh of his own sons. Hidden within the pollution we make and the denatured foods that we eat, a Greek god chuckles over his own vendetta.

One confirmation of all this comes from the progress of AIDS. After years of ameliorative measures, high-risk sexual behavior is once again on the rise. This is no longer due to a lack of information, however, but rather to *a reduced perception of what time means*. Young people today are aware of the risks. But because of the long latency period of the illness, the invalid that they might become at the age of 50 lies too far off in the future for them to care; they do not give it a second thought, because it is something *other*, incapable of eliciting their concern.

Our attitude towards human reality is marked by this ruinous lack of trust in continuity. We have come to realize that we can now destroy the human race not only with weapons, but also—for the first time—with environmental changes that could also destroy our unborn children.

Greek drama, that sacred enactment, was the opposite of the reduction of the temporal horizon brought about by entertainment. It penetrated time's depths, and compelled one to reflect on antecedents to the present and on the causality woven into our historical being. (Not by chance, those who ruled in those times commissioned works that would be completed only centuries after their death.)

Today, television, cinema, blockbuster shows, and advertising campaigns habituate us to distractions and the avoidance of thinking, because all of these are pastimes: indeed, they help us avoid awareness of the passage of time, of the fact that each hour notices and calls out to us.

Even economic life, necessarily organized in ever more complex sequences of time, tends to be seen and evaluated with reference only to the horizon of the present.[13] The discounting of performance is always asking what time it is, as the drug addict or the bulimic does. Even the value identified as a "future," in reality reduces a future value to one in the present. Paradoxically, only the present exists, eliminating the future in spite of its proud name—just as that thing called *tele*-vision (far-vision) reveals, on close inspection, the death of vision.

Continuity with the future is under attack but has not been done away with completely. It always gets back at us by breaking in with its own tragic outcomes. The discovery of a tumor cracks open the shell of time, dividing it in two. The time before diagnosis, with the gods under control, transforms into that non-time that psychiatry has called "waiting"[14]: a chronology without life, because imagination, educated by the simplistic canons of Hollywood, now manages to construe time as livable and meaningful only if it is that of a healthy, efficiently functioning, possibly well-off person. And in these few lines of ours we can barely note a fact that has been the object of the most important research[15]: namely, how the ill or dying person—once the protagonist of solemn processes—has become *reduced to the object of technologies* over which he has increasingly lost control, and the dying person has become so dehumanized or reduced that he has become taboo, a taboo which in the 20th century has taken the place held by sex in the 19th century.[16]

Jung has subjected Freud to criticism for his physiological and naturalistic view of analysis, through which creative efforts (in Sophocles, Leonardo, and Goethe) can be reduced to expressions of pathology.[17] The ancient gods—as Jung has said more than once—at first were reduced to dry abstractions, but today have changed into illnesses.[18]

Turning the page to the 21st century, psychoanalysis has been even further *reduced to psychotherapy*: to an exclusive preoccupation with illness, and therefore restricted to the time necessary for its cure. At bottom, those who practice this kind of therapy are afraid of intelligence, even of sympathy with themselves, which would demand that they embrace the human being in all of its temporal totality and depth.

Therefore, I would like to remind you of an ancient Greek drama that already recognized the convenience of reductivism, but with the aim of rejecting it.

In *Antigone*, Sophocles set forth the drama of the two sons and two daughters of Oedipus. Polynices has died in the assault on Thebes. Eteocles has likewise died defending the city. King Creon decrees that the body of Polynices be left to be eaten by crows, while that of Eteocles will be buried with military honors. The two sisters are quite different as well. Ismene dutifully obeys the laws, which in those days meant whatever the adamant king might decree: "I am powerless, she says, "against the state" (l. 79). But Antigone remembers that ever since human beings came into their proper humanity, the foundational custom has been the burial of one's own dead. The royal decree amounts to no more than a capricious ruling, a secondary affair that reduces itself to circumstances and takes account of only one of the brothers.

Antigone buries Polynices secretly. On discovering this, King Creon condemns her to be buried alive. Just as in her debate with Ismene, Antigone here stands irreconcilable against Creon. Antigone respects "the laws which are not for a day, nor for yesterday, but forever" (l. 452). And, if such respect is the same through time, then also the dead—people of the past—must receive the same respect that one gives to the living. For the king as well as for Ismene this attitude is incomprehensible. Time for them is merely the day at hand, and society is a village; they pay attention only to what surrounds them.

Confronted with the fate of Antigone, Creon's son Haemon, who loves her, kills himself. Then, out of despair, Haemon's mother

Eurydice, the king's wife, also takes her own life. Creon, who believed that he had won his struggle, remains alone and desperate. At the conclusion of the drama it is clear that the only real justice at work was Antigone's.

The unconscious fantasy of the society in which Sophocles lived expresses itself here quite clearly. An ethics that reduces itself to rules (to *governability*, as Lagos would say) renders life false to itself from within. The dead within the king himself symbolize what now has no future—what he gives birth to, his own son. Antigone is buried alive, which is to say that justice, although shut away from sight, continues to breathe. When the good dwindles and withers away, reducing itself to mere norms, the cure for such illness calls for the autonomy of the ordinary citizen who confronts the ruler of the state, or of the woman who stands up to the man, or of inspiration taking its stand in the face of unbending regulations. And all those buried alive with Antigone, even they are against Ismene.

CHAPTER SIX

The Clash of Civilizations? A Struggle between Identity and Functionalism

Paranoia, Mania, Civilization, and Functionalism

Among several disconcerting titles by Elias Canetti is *Die gespaltene Zukunft* (1972). The schizoid or "dissociated future" of which Canetti speaks refers both to a psychic and a cultural condition. His text sounds the following keynote:

> The times now approaching us are unprecedented. They are coming at us faster, and we are more conscious of making them happen. Their dangers and hopes are our own doing. The future is split, into destruction and a better life. Both of these tendencies are in train, whether in the world or in us.[1]

Canetti identified two branches of civilization that collide, but already in 1972 he said that they stem from the same trunk, and that the outcome of the battle depends on Western man and globalization.

Why do problems become inextricably political and psychological? Because the times speed up not only urgency but also complexity. They call for increasingly decisive solutions but also ever more complex mediations. This contradiction proves to be more intractable than the agony of our environment, and the temptation toward mental escape simply mounts. Hypermodernity, as Canetti remarks, compresses events but also mental processes; the mind suffocates beneath urgency, even if that feeling is not necessarily conscious. And whoever is suffocating, of course, thinks only of the next breath. Widespread problems fall into neglect, separated from the subject and fobbed off onto an adversary. These processes of flight and projection correspond to those forms of psychopathology known as *mania* and *paranoia*.

Complexities, however, are increasing far more than conflicts.[2] It is our need for flight from new complexities that simplifies them, presenting them as *clashes*. A good example might be the fact that the population of New York City, a concentration of American hegemonic power, will soon be only one quarter white, and WASP perhaps by only 10 to 15 percent.[3]

Maniacal flight and paranoid projection of responsibility are of interest to psychiatry only in extreme cases. In history, however, they are the stuff of daily life and the roots of most human conflicts. In the primitive scapegoat ritual a group assigns evil to one of its members or to an animal (often a goat), who is cast out and sacrificed. According to René Girard,[4] this practice of purification seamlessly splices the tribal world with European history. What we fear most deeply is not diversity but its opposite, the indefinite. We want to define difference, in order to fight it and expel it. To single out a symbolic carrier of evil is to *reinforce our identity* (we shall return to this problem presently). This archaic group self-therapy is paradoxically essential to our own day, because frantic economic and social changes—and the conversion of human relationships into virtual phantasms by new technology[5]—feed anxiety about identity; and this drives people to seek out a scapegoat. The current fashion, which believes itself to be infinitely removed from tribal paranoia as well as its perverse Hitlerian and Stalinist re-creations, in reality sustains them daily in a soft version (for example in "reality" TV shows).[6]

About the concepts of culture and civilization, James Hillman has remarked, "Culture flowers, Civilization works."[7] *Culture*, from the Latin, points to cultivation, through continuity with and growth of roots. Therefore, it pays due respect to natural cycles, such as the growing season. It holds to values that live in its past (the soil) and aims at conserving them in the future. Culture cannot indulge in mania because it must confer *identity*, by remaining stable through time. Civilization, by contrast, is instrumental and neutral. Like technology but unlike nature, it is able to make leaps, and by leaping it wounds the roots of identity. Civilization gives us *functionalism.* It heeds utility, not values. This clash, within us and without, is perhaps the most profound and true opposition that we must deal with.

The continual increase in functional demands coming our way instills panic; we fear losing our identity forever, but we do so unconsciously, limiting ourselves to rearranging the cyclone of the moment. Failing to make ourselves responsible over the long term, we insure that anxiety becomes permanent. To free ourselves from these demands we speed up the processes of maniacal escape and paranoid projection. This reactivity in its turn is functional, for it serves no purpose other than banishing responsibility into the provinces of space and time.

In the view of analytical psychology, the psyche functions through pairs of opposites. The negation that is intensified by embracing one aspect of a polarity (for example, between masculine and feminine) cannot simplify the dyad that they compose, and sooner or later leads to the return of the repressed in a pathological form. When the West too firmly excluded the feminine from its values, it was reborn in the hideous fantasy of the witch.

The disturbance that psychiatry calls manic-depressive disorder matches up with the dissociation between two absolutely natural psychic functions (as long as they remain balanced): activity and reflection. The word *mania* derives from an Indo-European root that simply means mental activity, and that stands behind any number of modern terms, such as the English *mind.* But the Western mind nevertheless is tempted to run to excess, and so these terms can also mean runaway thinking (in ancient Greek *maìnomai*) and agitation (*exmania*). This characteristic swerve of the West in comparison with the East implies a mentality that prefers external objects, overrides intervals of rest, and fills up free time. Not only do external events come at us more quickly, as Canetti has said, but these psychic processes accelerate themselves. The Western mind also suffers from juvenility, because the young are quick and older minds require deliberation. Therefore, in our communications media the world goes on presenting itself as young, even though we know from statistics that on average the population of the West is the oldest since the birth of humanity.

Paranoia, in turn, is the *moral expression* of maniacal hurry. The mind makes no allowances for periods of doubt, and so it preventatively assigns to others either specific evils or imagined wicked intentions.

One consequence is that a person with this mentality is likely to attack others immediately to head off their "intentions."

At the opposite pole to mania stands depression. Its most notable cultural expression has been melancholy. For centuries, melancholy has nourished the visual arts, music, and poetry. But the postmodern world, obsessed with instant responses in real time, sees depression and melancholy above all as diseases. Their typical mental spaces frame progressions in slow rhythm, are introverted, and are given to doubt and various shades of guilt. To eliminate these as being dysfunctional and unproductive is to reject one's responsibility for oneself and, in a vicious circle, to enhance paranoia.

By worshipping haste, and refusing those feelings of responsibility that are born from doubt, we have irreversibly broken up the bipolar equilibrium between two psychologies, the manic-paranoid and the depressive-reflective. This European contagion—through imperialism, colonialism, and globalization—has infected the whole world.

Self-Limitation and Culture

At the origins of Western thought, the Greeks, being reflective, practiced the art of self-limitation. Aristotle criticized those who would enlarge the state; its optimal population size was never to exceed the number that could be reached by a public speaker's voice.[8] Anything larger would result in people knowing each other less well and this would weaken their common life. The unlimited growth of the state—our own condition today—is a function of power inimical to identity. Giving in to the temptation of growth, the state swells with foreigners. We may also interpret Aristotle's concern symbolically: with inordinate growth, not only does a country fill itself with immigrants but the collective mentality accumulates too many new contents. The foreigner inevitably becomes the otherness internal to a country's workings, just as a suspect notion inevitably turns into the mind's other; in this way identity (which the foreign presence places in doubt) and functionalism (which population growth enhances) oppose each other. Aristotle obviously did not invoke the scapegoat, but he would have found himself in agreement with Girard. Sooner or later the contrast will be projected onto some neighboring country or onto a different culture and driven out, activating on a local scale the "clash of civilizations."

Already in the 5th century B.C.E. the respect for limits was infected by its opposite: the Greeks defeated the grandiosity of the Persian Empire, but then, following suit, they began to feel grandiose themselves. First Athens, then Macedonia, then Rome changed over to an expansive mentality, which had reached them from the Eastern mentality. The seeds of mania and paranoia became scattered throughout the world.

Something analogous happened with religion. A maniacal expansiveness (evident in the hyperactive Paul of Tarsus) shattered the equilibrium of psychic opposites. Christianity invented mission efforts and proselytism, aimed at increasing the demographics of the faithful. A few hundred years later another new branch of Hebraic-like monotheism showed up on the Arabian peninsula and sought expansion. From this perspective, the greater part of the historical conflicts between Islam and Christianity are intramural Western affairs, stemming from expansive tendencies established long since. Obviously, the two World Wars, also known as "Europe's civil wars," were purely internal to our psychic equilibrium, as was the Cold War.

We are talking, therefore, about the Western world in the largest sense. Likewise, the duel between Christianity and Islam—the "civil war of monotheism"—and that between left and right, between capitalism and communism (if communism ever existed: many have maintained that it has never been tried on the grounds that after World War II very few so-called communist countries had actual communist societies), are tendencies *internal* to this secular swerve toward mania and paranoia.

Naturally, an alternative mental model has always existed, which Democritus anticipated with his dictum, "It is better to correct one's own errors than those of others."[9] Bertrand Russell diagnosed the Western malady as a "Byronic unhappiness," which is to say a frenzy condemned to permanent dissatisfaction. A background chorus of wisdom supports this view, but in the West these insights have never constituted a mass culture. This reflective attitude, in the modern epoch, has had to look to the Enlightenment and to psychology for reinforcement. Paradoxically, however, in the last few decades the self-assumed responsibility for sustaining psychic equilibrium seems to have regressed, owing to the effects of mass merchandising and mass communication; both of these agencies habituate people only to external objects and to ready access and assimilation.

To be sure, it is not possible to reduce history to a conflict between a maniacal, expansive West and a reflective rest of the world. China, for example, was constantly tempted by grandiosity. Seventy-five years before the discovery of America, Admiral Zheng He already had at his disposal a fleet of several hundred ships and tens of thousands of sailors, which he aimed westward. Columbus commanded less than a hundred men and three caravels, the smallest of which was only as long as the Chinese flagship's rudder. It is interesting to observe that although Western writers note that such expeditions could have initiated world conquest,[10] the Chinese themselves say they served above all to strengthen the honor and prestige of the empire.[11]

All the same, while Zheng He was under sail, back at the court in Peking the Mandarin faction, in every sense representing culture and national identity (these high functionaries achieved their positions through difficult examinations in classical literature, not in administrative matters), defeated the Eunuch faction (the party of activism, functionality, and immediate results). Lightning started large fires in the Forbidden City, and this precipitated a round of contentious and arcane debates: presumably heaven was not in full harmony with emperor Zhu Di, perhaps because he had engaged in too many cyclopean undertakings. When the emperor died, his successors adopted policies that forcibly closed China. Naturally, merchants suffered (foreign trade was straightaway condemned as piracy), but they were not the priority. China sealed its borders.

What happened in Europe also cannot be simplified too readily. In the following century, there developed in Spain the greatest theological battle of all time. The conquest of the Americas set off a contest between an imperialistic theology, according to which the natives did not have souls or were naturally inferior, and a nativist theology (propounded by Bartolomé de Las Casas and Francisco de Vitoria), according to which the native peoples were the equals of Europeans. Nativist theologians won the debates and laid out the legislative basis for relations with the colonies, anticipating modern international law. While discussions were taking place in Spain, however, and affirming those abstractions—those "useless passions" of the Europeans—in America, the first and greatest genocide in history was carried out. Europe lacked the equilibrium of the ancient East; utilitarian expansion—civilization, ho!—proved to be far stronger than accommodation to a culture and its values.

When it reflects on its antecedents, therefore, our postmodern viewpoint can observe a dramatic contest between identity (the Mandarins defending China, or the great theologians Las Casas and Vitoria standing up for native peoples) and functionalism, which, dispensing with values, gives absolute precedence to conquest, an accumulation of means that still have not settled the problem of their ends. As we know, over time values grow weak; in the epoch we have surveyed, military, economic, and technical developments have imposed themselves on morals. Spanish law declared natives the equals of Europeans, but in the colonies, a few friars were faced with an ever-growing number of adventurers and immigrants, and an immense array of commercial interests.

China, along with Japan, which closed its borders 200 years later, succeeded in barricading their identities for a long time, but today they are mounting a maniacal Western relay race.

Clashes and Goats

In the final decade of the last century, Francis Fukuyama defined the fall of the Berlin Wall and the end of the Cold War as *The End of History.* While the history that has followed has lodged its dissent, it remains true that the '90s were a privileged period, exceptionally free of paranoia. The projection of evil onto an absolute enemy no longer prevailed. Conflicts seemed to migrate back along the dry branches of geography and history, into the Balkans or Africa; it seemed that the era was busy selling them off like out-of-date goods on the counter at a supermarket. A transatlantic collective unconscious saw them, by that time, as postmodern versions of Kipling's white man's burden: not as mortal challenges to the West, but as confirmations of its superiority, for which only a small price had to be paid.

It was a unique period during which, in the absence of major challenges, the West would have been able directly to assume global responsibility for the environment, disarmament, and the defense of cultural identity. That is, attention could have focused not on partial disputes and their brief intervals but on chronic themes, which call for unrelenting self-criticism: the depressive but profound psychology of Chronos.

If the '90s were "easy" from the viewpoint of international economics and politics, they were nonetheless psychologically difficult for the West, constrained as it was to an equilibrium extraneous to its habitual functioning. Our mentality is accustomed to a maniacal rhythm and tempo, and to the projection of responsibility; a pause for reflection can seem to fall like some random impediment on the street down which we are running. Unconsciously, we look for some new scapegoat and some new enemy to hunt down.

The collective unconscious imagination, therefore, heaved a sigh of relief with the arrival of September 11, 2001. The mass media in the new century have been able to galvanize into life once again all the old mental reaction patterns of the Cold War, transformed into *The Clash of Civilizations* that Samuel Huntington has erected as a counter-façade to *The End of History*, to the point where we might call his manifesto "the restoration of history." Altogether it amounts to a return of history with ideology; the media rolled out the political manifesto drafted long before in the '90s by the right-wing Republican PNAC (Project for a New American Century), which proposed American supremacy as its program.[12]

The vision of the future promoted in this document adopts the mental perspectives of the past, but overlooks two fundamental facts: (1) The radical attack on "American civilization" is symbolic and media-framed, not military; it would call first of all for a commitment to the psychology of symbols, and only secondarily for a strengthened military role; (2) the struggle no longer pits the United States against a revolutionary movement or an Evil Empire, easily identified with what is beyond the Iron Curtain, but (if these distinctions have any meaning) against a reactionary religious vision bent on restoring a mythical past and a theocratic society, scattered like the leopard's spots across the globe. Today the battle is asymmetrical both in time and space. This second aspect combines with the first. From the pharaohs to Bush Junior, no theocracy has been subdued solely by military means. The Aztec Empire, for example, far stronger militarily than the invading Spaniards, crumbled when Montezuma was no longer able to feel his divine status and was shot by his own subjects.[13]

In essence, the American government (and in its wake the entire media system of the West) has failed to take account of either factor. Through sheer inertia, the United States goes on laying out the greatest government military expenditure of all time. After September 12, 2001, military spending has only increased, and now amounts to nearly half of all military outlays in the world (or, as has been noted, around 30 times the amount that would meet the challenge of world hunger). In this dizzying number shines the absence of any attention to psychology.

From a psychological perspective, September 12, 2001 is more interesting than September 11. If the 11th is symbol, the 12th is panic, revealing our fear of that symbol, our estrangement from symbols, and the paranoid reaction and anti-psychological attitude of the principal actors. With September 12, 2001, the real encounter swims to the surface, entirely internal to Western civilization. Its stark contrast stands forth—between the unconscious, inflicting itself purely in the form of collective fantasies, and rationality, which sets out in lockstep to colonize the new century.

If we believe that a "clash of civilizations" has taken the West by surprise, then we have to ask why it might be surprised by anything at all, when marketing was entirely ready for it. In fact, however, the West has actually been accustomed to such collisions for a long time. The first description of a clash of civilizations comes in the 5th century B.C.E. The writer is known as Herodotus of Halicarnassus, and the book is called *The Histories.* Already, the first page of the initial episode (1.1-5) tells how the contrasts between East and West came about, attributing them to artificial exaggeration. And on the second page, Herodotus shakes his head over the futility of the conflict; in fact the whole thing comes down to a series of kidnappings of women, the second woman being named, significantly, Europa. "Abducting young women, in their opinion, is not, indeed, a lawful act; but it is stupid after the event to make a fuss about it. The only sensible thing is to take no notice; for it is obvious that no young woman allows herself to be abducted if she does not wish to be."[14] The father of history, besides establishing that misogyny is as old as history itself, demonstrates that history is a paranoid psychic contagion. It consists in coming down with a fever brought on by the "original paranoid event," from which everything else follows.

Pinning psychic error on an adversary lets me avoid confronting my own contradictions and evils; as their subject I simply assign them to an external *object* (Latin *ob-iectare*, against-throw). Thus does one denounce the crimes of a neighbor. This behavior changes the external object not only into a criminal, but also into a *permanent enemy.* It gives the appearance of dealing with evils as a moral task, but in substance it corrupts us in turn. We must confess that crime is more seductive than any other psychic principle, because we so readily make it our own. So long as we commit an evil act in response, it is good. But we also need to increase the dosage of evil, for now that the guilty party is also an enemy one must obtain *not only justification, but victory.* Throughout the chapters of Book One, Herodotus identifies the virus of the historical process as *tísis* or retributive, vengeful justice. Circulating in society and history, the individual psychic infection becomes collective and permanent, just as an individual bacterial infection can mutate into an epidemic, and then into endemic conditions. In this way, Herodotus wrote, Asia and Europe began to invest their energies in successive campaigns of self-ruination, instead of enjoying the civilization that they had already brought to flower. Within one generation, the ugly practice of rape had become so contagious that one Eastern prince, Paris of Troy, loaded his baggage with Helen and, confident that he would get away with it just as the Greeks had done (*Histories* 1.3), brought on the most famous conflict of all time, the Trojan War.

Continental battles—the most intense eruptions of this volcano—run through our history, from Herodotus to Huntington, with a clear response, the simplest one. Even when brushed by catastrophe, Europe managed to exercise overwhelming military superiority. In 490 B.C.E., when the Persians attacked Athens and met the hoplite infantry spears of the Greek militia, they lost 33 times as many men as the Greeks did. Twenty-two centuries later, in 1683, the Polish cavalry of King Jan Sobieski with one stroke smashed the siege of Vienna and the secular expansion of the Ottoman Turks, killing around 15,000 troops in a few hours.

The West has won all these historic encounters but, as Nietzsche and then Spengler have warned, it is as though the West lost a decisive battle with its victory. Gradually, in recent generations, and at a dizzying pace in the last few years, Western society has become unbalanced by history. For the first time it has conquered hunger, but also for the first time it grows sick from too much food. Its citizens need not fear external enemies who would take their lives, but growing numbers of them take their own lives. (In fact, due to propaganda, Western citizenries are often unnecessarily afraid.) The civilization that has subdued the hazards of the natural environment is the same that has turned itself, unnaturally so, into the greatest of hazards for the survival of the environment.

A similar dilemma, which is perfectly clear to psychology and anthropology, is almost impossible to translate into the language of the mass media. The theoretical catch-phrase "clash of civilizations" simplifies it, rendering it visible, exiling it for as long as possible to the outside, like the longed-for goat. It is no longer the traditional duel between neighboring countries, but one between distant civilizations, separated by geography as well as developmental age, panicked into flight by every kind of anxiety because *they are too close.* The whole matter is a continuation of the Western tradition of exporting its internal problems in the form of colonialist enterprise.

In the collective imagination of the West, the clash of civilizations is a narrative continuation of the conflict between Asia and Europe framed by Herodotus: an archaic fact that, like certain childhood nightmares, traumatically returns at the prompting of certain surface details. What is new in all this, with acknowledgement to Huntington, is its *systematic and eschatological deployment*: the media mobilization of the public through menacing shocks delivered to the global masses. In sum, the new thing is not the clash of civilizations but the cultivation of clashes.

The narrative of September 12—namely, the crusade and revenge of the West—was there all along, pre-existent in the unconscious and gathering force and autonomous dynamism. It absorbed these elements from centuries and millennia of our culture, and a reality of this nature cannot subsist without having consequences. The myths of vengeance, set aside by official culture, do not simply disappear; rather, they show up as pathological eruptions, more or less in the manner of a dormant volcano that sometimes turns active. In the terms that the mass media render banal, two very different things—the clash of civilizations and *the narrative of September 12*—are identified with each other. September 11, 2001 is *the date of a calamitous event, but not of a new civilizational conflict.* Instead, a new narrative gets under way,[15] which has no small consequences: to mention only one among many, an altered relationship between the two continents flanking the North Atlantic.

In the global scenario, the paranoid style of fear has agreed to declare war against not an enemy but an abstraction (*the war on terror*) and an invisible adversary (*faceless enemy*). On the inner plane, the scapegoat is the immigrant group (attracted by a business community that seeks cheap labor, but that also might finance right-wing movements that demand the expulsion of immigrants). Naturally the perfect synthesis is achieved when immigrant and terrorist become one and the same.

We can almost formulate it axiomatically: any idea can be sold, in paranoid terms, if the mass media successfully reduce the adversary's attitude to a threat to identity. The populace trains its eyes on the scapegoat, forgetting that the same brand was eagerly snapped up many years earlier simply to maintain the semblance of ever growing vitality. In Switzerland, which, thanks to prosperity, has been flooded with guest-worker immigrants for decades, Max Frisch was the first to observe sarcastically: "What a terrible thing! We called for manual laborers, and instead we got people!"

Let us return to "Canetti's dilemma." As for the continual erosion of self-criticism in a society gripped by haste and consumerism, we reject with increasing force any conflict among the alternatives that are possible *to us*. We project our psychological dilemmas into conflicts outside ourselves, leaving ourselves to stand for what is right. To return to the example quoted earlier, we do not look at the potential conflicts internal to ethnic groups in New York City, but at the clash of Islam with the West. Making our daily concessions to functionalism, we renew the Faustian bargain of the soul in a postmodern way. This blindness comes at a tremendous cost and, as an accessory to globalization, now affects every country.

Let us take an example: hunger is age-old, whether in India or Brazil (in treating quite different countries, we would do well to approach certain problems as common ones). New economic development is now rapidly placing more calories at the disposal of those countries. But, just as this premodern problem finds resolution, a postmodern one explodes, with no capability on the part of statistics to pigeonhole it: tens of millions of citizens of India and Brazil already are overweight. Without having had time to escape famine, already we are prisoners of overeating. Because it is children above all who are affected, in a few years obesity will strike like a cultural form of AIDS. In these same countries, too, consumption has already swollen beyond actual need.

The availability of food, unfortunately, grows through *functional* means that operate at the expense of *identity*. The excesses of functionalism, in turn, are part and parcel of maniacal *hybris*, without either object or end, truly a psychic infection that emerging nations import from the West. The industrialization of agriculture eliminates the family vegetable garden and accelerates the disappearance of tasks related to agriculture, as well as their communities. Culture (in both senses of the word) is vanishing, and nothing is arising to replace it. To produce food and to live from that practice were always both ritual and culture, that is, they have always constituted values and identity in themselves. The raising of calories without culture—without sowing seed, protecting growing plants, and celebrating the rituals of harvest—starves the human psyche.

Let me close with another example, this time pertaining to the West.

The American Medical Association (AMA) has taken a stand on the interrogations of detainees at Guantánamo (the modern American "Statue of Anti-Liberty"). Whatever the interrogations are called—whether the word *torture* is used or not—they cause suffering and therefore violate the Hippocratic oath. The AMA defends the millennial cultural identity of the physician, with no concessions whatsoever made to *functionalism*. In contrast, the American Psychological Association (APA) has splintered over the question. The "psychological technique of interrogation," with all its attendant torments, has seemed to many in this group a neutral business,[16] something that should manage to reach its goal of defending America and its values. Instead, the country's own historical identity, represented by the Constitution (its Fourth, Fifth, and Sixth Amendments), has come to be sacrificed, like a scapegoat, to the golem of functionalism.

The suspension of law in order to reach political objectives more quickly had already extinguished the comet that burned across the 20th century, the one named Communism. If the triumph of the West amounts to the triumph of maniacal functionalism and the rejection of responsibility, then the real struggle has already been lost, even for the liberal democracies. It is significant that their prototype, the United States of America, is defined predominantly not as a state but as an activity: *the American way of life*. That operational definition does not propose a goal or a purpose, but a way, a road, a function, a means[17]: just as *war* (*on terror*) and *clash* (*of civilizations*) are only movements, not destinations.

Worshipping success as such (regardless of whether it be economic or military), the West has also mistaken a means for an end. But the

West, in accepting the continual change that comes with utilitarianism, feels untrue to itself and chips away at its own identity. In this way it condemns itself always to seek out new conflicts, as screens onto which to project its bad faith.

CHAPTER SEVEN

Almachius and the Demon: Mass Entertainment and Violence-as-Spectacle

Populu' studio stupidus in funambulo / animum occuparat.
[The populace, stupefied with amazement, lost themselves to a tightrope-walker.]

—Terence, *Hecyra / The Mother-in-law*,
Prologue I, ll. 4-5

At Dodona, lying beyond the tourist traffic that has vulgarized Greece, is a sanctuary dedicated to Zeus. Nearby, as was customary in ancient cult practice, shielded by woods and rocks, stands a theater.

Among the few items of information known with any certainty, one will strike the visitor. Having become masters of the place, the Romans revived the theater. But they adapted it to their own uses: with only the slightest modifications, they transformed it into a stage for combat, between animals, or between animals and men, or between gladiators. The same thing happened in many other parts of conquered Greece. Cities such as Corinth came to have two structures intended for these games. In some theaters the bottom was tinned watertight to allow flooding for the staging of naval battles.[1]

In Greece the theater served the enactment of dramas, that is, dialogues between characters. Performances went on throughout the day. Engagement and communication with the public were intense and profound. Thinking about the problem of good and evil was the most important task. But it was also understood that people are unable to carry on in this way without a break, and so, after three tragedies they were treated to a comedy. After a day at the theater, the audience went home satisfied and thoughtful. Tragedy declares that the presence of evil cannot be eliminated. Yet neither can one eliminate the need to do battle with it. It is through this unavoidable struggle that evil—as Jacob learned[2]—can transform itself into a messenger.

A human being has many demons within. We still meet up with them at night in our dreams. The quickening of the imagination in the theater made it possible for one to get to know them, but it also kept them under control; it was a form of teaching, a kind of education. That exacting moralist Plato distrusted the theater and epic poetry because they gave people pleasure. And yet it was an edifying kind of pleasure, the enjoyment of wisdom. The real problem would come later, when Roman practices began to popularize sheer spectacle, which gave free rein to passions and had nothing to do with education.

A commonplace has it that Roman civilization was conquered by that of Greece.[3] Nonetheless, for anyone who considers spectacles (today known as the mass media) and their essential civic and educational function, the opposite occurred. This cultural catastrophe has been passed over in silence, because the official history of the West must uphold its arrogant faith in progress. Behaving in this way, the West has, since Late Antiquity, made a habit of minimizing its regressions.

Although my argument here is brief, it must still review a bit of linguistic and theatrical history at this point, if we are to become more conscious of the irreversible development that affects us so deeply. It is a matter of slowing down enough to absorb a shift in consciousness. The Latin noun *spectaculum*, and its derivatives in modern Romance languages, come from the verb *specio*, which originally meant "to look," with many active implications. Likewise, the Greek noun *theatron* stems from the verb *theaomai*, which also means "to look," in the manner of contemplation, with faith or belief (*theos* is a god, and *theoros* is someone who carries out a religious function). In time, *specio* spliced itself with *specto* (leading precisely to *spectaculum*), and the active sense allied with "assist," "be a spectator." A similar process took place with *theatron* in Greek. Theater is born as a religious event, and, as is often the case with religious rituals, with time the public separates from the celebrants, more disposed to witnessing than to performing.

And on that fact swings the hinge of irreversibility. The degeneration into passivity of what was originally active (*spectare* and *theaomai*) is even clearer in the Germanic languages. The English *show* has the same root as the German *schauen* (Italian *guardare*, or look), but today it has come to mean that what is looked at is seen not actively but passively. Likewise, in contemporary German, the spectacle is a *Schau-spiel* (literally, as in English, a *play* made to be seen; a tragedy, accordingly, is a *Trauerspiel*). Spectacle and theater were originally the same thing, but they were both implicitly understood to function actively. This function, however, is performed in a different way when the goals of society and the state change. In classical Athens, at least ideally, along the lines of *eu-nomia*, spectacles were turned toward the good, and they compensated citizens for their hardship: Pericles, in his funeral oration for the war dead, boasts, "We have not forgotten to provide for our weary spirits many relaxations from toil ... and the delight which we daily feel in all these things helps us to banish melancholy."[4] Imperial Rome, by contrast, had already turned toward *Realpolitik*, born as a means stripped of ideals: authority chained itself to the obligation to provide sufficient amusement or pastimes for the populace, along with the imperative of amassing the necessary food.[5]

That step removes any trace of dialectic from the relationship between the people and power. It transforms that relationship into a rigid symbiosis, in which spectacle functions as a means of social control, binding the parties in mutual dependence. This imperialism without ideals anticipates modern times, in which citizens are passive and the mass medium of bad quality is as necessary to the public as it is to power. Both end up mutually and permanently ensnared in decadent spectacle. The fact that the words "spectacle" and "theater" originally indicated an activity of the public but finally degenerated into indicating its passivity is therefore highly significant, and links up with their drift towards violence and pornography. The meaning of speech inverts itself when the purposes that let citizens join together turn upside-down. Greek theater or spectacle aimed at moving the public to think about the problem of good and evil. Its successors—beginning with the Roman circus—for the most part wanted the masses not to think, preferring them to leave all decisions about good and evil to the authorities.

Within a few years after the arrival of the Romans, theater and public spectacle had become something radically different. Whereas the Greek form, as psychoanalysis would say today, strengthened ego structure, deepening and containing its relation to the unconscious, the Roman circus weakened the ego, placing it at the mercy of uncontrollable and primordial passions.

Like the Greeks, the Romans greatly enjoyed public spectacles. Also like the Greeks, they appreciated theatrical productions. Unlike them, however, they staged these productions in flimsy, smaller buildings, and preferred comedies to tragedies. But the real Roman spectacle was combat in the arena, inspired by other cultures, above all the Etruscans. The premiere of a play by a major Roman author, Terence, was broken off, as he tells us,[6] because the audience learned that a circus spectacle was opening, and they poured out of the theater.

The circus, as its name indicates, was a circular construction on a huge scale. From the architectural point of view, it doubled the semicircle of the traditional Greek theater plan, producing an amphitheater surrounding an arena. The grand scale was due to the fact that the events drew huge crowds. The circular form of the circus was necessitated by the fact that it also had to accommodate horse races; a hippodrome must be circular or elliptical.

Entertainments were alternated and, as in Greece, for the most part filled out the course of a day of festival. At their height during the heyday of the Roman Empire, holidays numbered nearly 200 a year. As the populace had the right to take part freely, historians have not hesitated to claim that the circus contributed its share to Roman decadence.

A typical day at the games went as follows.[7] The morning was devoted to wild animal fights, with each other or with human beings. The scenery might include rocks, trees, and sand, to evoke far-off places in the grand style. But the real marvel was the presence of exotic animals, especially from Africa. The beasts slaughtered in the Colosseum numbered in the thousands;[8] and it was no small matter, given the means available at the time, to secure an uninterrupted flow of fresh lions, bears, and hippos. At high noon, the arena was littered with blood and shreds of flesh, both animal and human.

The long lunch hour could be devoted to the meting out of capital punishments. This was not simply a matter of carrying out a legal procedure. The delivery of the condemned to execution was also a celebration of universal devotion to the state, established religion, and the emperor. The death or punishment of a condemned person was not just a concern of that person alone; it was an essential part of a public ritual in which civic authorities determined what was good and what was evil, solemnly asserting their monopoly on violence.[9] The myth of Prometheus played itself out literally. For in contrast to the simulation in Aeschylus's eponymous drama, the act of the eagle tearing the hero's liver to pieces became real, employing no mere actor but someone actually condemned to death, thus fulfilling two functions at once.[10] Just as our own times show us, extreme cruelty associates itself with extreme sex. A woman condemned to death enacts the myth of Pasiphae; at her execution she is gored by a bull.[11]

The afternoon was devoted to combats between gladiators, recruited from among those who had nothing to lose—slaves or prisoners of war. Like the races, these spectacles were the occasion for gambling and explosions of violent emotion in the crowd. We know from tradition that when one of the duelists was about to be killed, he could call for mercy by lifting his finger, and the spectators would roar their approval or condemnation. The final word, however, came from the organizer of the games.[12] The gladiator was trained not only to engage in mortal combat without giving quarter, but also to collaborate in the spectacle and play out to the end the role of the courageous fighter, concerned only with an honorable death. If he fell, but offered his throat disdainfully to the sword of his adversary, he stood the best possible chance of moving the spectators and staying alive. If he showed fear of dying, then he spoiled the show, and this would unleash furious reactions and a feeling of evil omen among the spectators, who would then cry out for his blood.[13] In brief, reality turned itself upside-down: *in order to live, the gladiator had to pretend that he wanted to die.* If instead—humanly and sincerely—he demonstrated a fear of dying, the spectators called for his death. In a manner not unlike ours today, the Roman public cried out for spectacles that compounded violence with sham.

To put it in modern terms, we could say that the circus was the chief means of communicating with the public, and the only mass medium, a fact that implied an all-pervasive culture of the spectacle.

What do wild animal fights, duels between man and beast, gladiatorial contests, mock naval battles, and public executions have in common? The natural answer that we would give today is that they all belong to a monoculture of cruelty and the turning of violence as an end in itself into sheer spectacle.

It is commonly said these days that spectacle devoid of purpose (recall Marshall McLuhan's adage, "the medium is the message")—stripped of story, dialogue, or edification—tends to degenerate into the glorification of violence and sex. But the human mind possesses primary foundations (archetypes) that the collective weight of historical circumstances can scarcely alter; this was as true back then as it is today. In contrast to theater, the "drama" that unfolded in the amphitheater had no transcendent meaning. The fight was purely physical; it was the struggle itself. The mob did not want to think about death; it wanted dead bodies. If most spectacles were bloody affairs, the festival in honor of Dea Flora, devoted to celebrating the renewal of the life cycle in the spring (April 28 - May 3), came down to theatrical shows in which the performers were prostitutes (persons already condemned, not to dying a violent death, but to giving up ownership of their bodies). The public, in fact, would quickly tire of the theatrics and begin to raise a clamor, demanding that the women strip off their clothes. In variations on this routine, the actresses, in order not to waste any time, would come on stage already stripped. Even so, at bottom, the spectacle was more violent than erotic in substance: it gave vent to the sadism of a pack of males out after their prey, much like the "hunting scenes" gruesomely reproduced in the Colosseum.

We ought to reflect on the particular cruelty of the crowd when it called for the death of the gladiator who showed fear of dying. It would appear that the terrified man's action marked an exit from the bubble, a return to terrible human reality. This posed a problem in that it threw back upon the spectators a primordial feeling of guilt, a sense of responsibility for the shedding of that blood—a guilt they immediately got rid of through projection, shouting for it to be silenced once and for all. The situation is not that alien to us moderns. Of course, we do not produce nearly as much direct cruelty in the form of spectacle as the Romans did, but we do reproduce it in stories or documentaries devoted to war and crime in movies and on television. Every now and then, one of these modern shows veers off the main path (in entertainment, the fairytale groove of happy killing and dying) and takes us in a critical direction; it offers "scandal," showing war for what it really is—gratuitously exaggerated horror and torture—and challenging us to renounce needless suffering. But such films or television shows have a difficult time finding a "market." It is much easier for the mass audience to ignore them, or reject them, as it did with the gladiator who, crying for mercy, stirred up a bad conscience.

The human animal produced by evolution is perfectly adapted to living in small groups, not much different from the apes. Within such groups, humans, like animals, are subject to natural mechanisms that set limits on aggressive behavior. But in complex societies and in large masses, these natural processes are no longer able to operate; the limits on human violence have to be set by culture. In this respect, public spectacle constitutes a watershed: going down one side of the mountain it enters into containment; going down the other it goes forth and multiplies.

True and proper theater is a means of communication. But it is quite a different matter to inculcate piety and wisdom in many minds individually at once. No means of *mass* communication has ever served that purpose. In Ancient Greece there was no explicit provision for a real education, whether religious, moral, or civic. It was theatrical spectacle above all that accomplished this task, and, at least in Athens, did so exceptionally well. Each tragedy showed that evil has always lived within human beings, independently of their intentions. Educated in this truth, citizens were able to develop the capacity for introspection and self-criticism, much more so than they have been in any other period in history—and, paradoxically, more thoroughly than in our day, which articulates, at least theoretically, a new kind of knowing assigned specifically to self-knowledge, namely, psychoanalysis.

Those societies that achieved a certain fragile cultural harmony through the use of drama succeeded, in a certain measure, in *containing* evil, albeit as much in collective consciousness as in the individual psyche; in nearly every other case, society has done little more than *repress* it. Ever since the Ancient Greeks, this kind of cultural harmony has survived only by serving purposes less inclusive than the containment of evil. In recent centuries, for the most part, theater has degenerated into simple *entertainment.* Geniuses such as Shakespeare and Goethe (and to some extent Racine and Corneille) were able to revive certain aspects of ancient Greek dramatic action, but without being able to ensure their future in the West. In particular, theater since their time has not been the total experience that it was in Sophocles' day, no longer affording a total experience viewed by the entire populace. Classical Athenian society constituted, therefore, a brief departure from the norm. On a limited scale, and focusedinternally on a leap towards the wisdom and utopia promised by the sophists and philosophers, the population of classical Athens came together not simply to pass the time, but in order to improve themselves.[14] Uniquely similar conditions in the course of Western history have kept at bay the demons that live within us.

Never in human history has an angel fallen so rapidly. With the Romanization of the Mediterranean world, spectacle—the meeting point and the moment of encounter among citizens, the very form of their public and communal life—plunges, in the blink of an eye, from the heaven of tragedic wisdom into the hell of cruelty, where pleasure is given over to violence.

The most revolutionary ethical and religious renewal in the West began with Jesus of Nazareth and, with the passage of two centuries, penetrated to the heart of the Roman Empire. At the beginning of the 4th century C.E., the emperor Constantine took action in view of the new reality, granting to Christianity the seal of approval of the establishment. But the populace, in which the new commandment of love had made its home, remained a poorly educated mass society. And the crowd, when it is set free from restraints, cut loose from responsibility, loves—perhaps more instinctively than anything else, even love itself—violence, love's opposite.

And so, around 100 years after Constantine, at the beginning of the last century of life remaining to it, Rome continued to go crazy over the blood and ferocity on display at the Colosseum.

That is when Almachius[15] makes his entrance on stage.

It may well have been God's voice that spoke to him and got him on the road. Almachius "led the ascetic life" in what was then the Eastern Empire, probably in present-day Syria.[16] As Theodoret writes, "he came to Rome in order to put a stop to gladiatorial combat." Of necessity, it took a very long time to cover such a distance, since he traveled mainly on foot, begging for alms along the way. But the interior word kept him company and helped him to remain firm in his resolve.

When he got to Rome, however, events unfolded in rapid succession. The monk "entered into the stadium [the Colosseum] and, descending into the arena, interposed himself between several of those who were fighting each other." This probably happened in 404 on the day that modern calendars mark as the 1st of January. According to the Martyrology of St. Jerome,[17] the monk cried out, "Today is the eighth day after the birthday of Our Lord—stop observing superstitious cults and the sacrifices they devise!" Naturally, Almachius had, in every sense, put himself on the spot. But the weapons of the gladiators, wedging him where he stood, did not strike him. Instead, Theodoret continues, "the *public* for this cruel spectacle, outraged, and *welcoming the frenzy of the demon that rejoiced in that blood*,[18] stoned and killed the bearer of peace."

In this stormy description, the psychic factors assume a personal character and become fundamental subjects. An ego that makes conscious decisions is absent among the spectators. They do not execute a choice but *passively welcome* a demon within the soul. And the *daimon*, in turn, takes pleasure in blood, actually feasting on it. When from the teats of this monster the spectators suck the milk of violence, a contagion arises among them, accompanied by another collapse; they go from the passive enjoyment of cruelty to the active enactment of it. Without being conscious of it, they return, in a perverse way, to the original sense of "spectacle," that of participation. They slip into this behavior without realizing it, with no change of emotion, with no awareness of responsibility, because the shock has broken like a wave over the crowd, and because the collective unconscious preserves a "memory of the theater" that is lost to consciousness under the simplifying influence of the passage of time. They become psychologically contaminated from witnessing the spectacle of killing; and then they kill. They welcome the demon that rejoices in blood; then they spill blood themselves.

In this account, Theodoret of Cyrus created a juxtaposition of extreme opposites in ethics. Almachius hears the voice of conscience. The spectators quite simply have no conscience whatsoever. Their soul is that Shakespearean hollow drained of signification and resonating only with *sound and fury*.[19]

Sixteen centuries later, on September 12, 2001 (a date significant because from that day on the West has known no peace, and wherever it perceives enemies it is pricked by its own bad conscience), Pedrito of Portugal descended into the arena. As we know, Portugal pursues bullfighting as avidly as Spain does, but without the killing of the bull. On that day, both the bulls and the matador were in exceptionally fine form, and the spectators were beside themselves with excitement. When Pedrito had worn down his third bull, they all got to their feet yelling, "*Mata, mata!*" Like the crowd, Pedrito yielded to impulse and thrust his sword into the animal's heart. Two years later, he was punished with a fine of 105,000 euros. Six years later, after a futile appeal before the Constitutional Tribunal, Pedrito was condemned "definitively."[20] But this point carries little weight, since he is now Portugal's most famous bullfighter and one of the most in demand in the world.[21] The fact of being "condemned" *to* violence seems, therefore, rather more "definitive" than being condemned *for* any single *act* of violence.

The historical and juridical contingencies owing to which the killing of the bull is prohibited in Portugal (or elsewhere) even though it is permitted in Spain (or elsewhere) are not to our point. What is interesting is the fact that there might come—as once upon a time there came in the Colosseum, in Spain, yesterday in Portugal (one of the most peaceful countries in the world), and may come tomorrow, maybe, in the piazza near one's house—a moment in which the people open themselves to this *daimon*, get to their feet, and yell, "Kill!" When will it happen, and why? In response to that furious demand from the crowd someone, sooner or later, will say *yes*, not necessarily out of wickedness, but simply for the sake of expediency.

A similar motive, transcending the differences of time and place, underlies the culminating episode of the ministry of Christ in the canonical gospels. At the Passover, one recalls, it was customary for the Roman governor of Palestine (though this is an unsubstantiated claim, perhaps used by the Evangelists to present their readers with a symbolic dilemma) to free a condemned man. Pontius Pilate presented the crowd with a choice between two prisoners. Matthew[22] adds that both were named Jesus: the first, Jesus Barabbas; the second, Jesus the Messiah (or the Christ, following the Greek). Things grow even more confusing when we consider that in Aramaic "Barabbas" means "son of the father," and that Jesus of Nazareth claimed to be the Son of the Heavenly Father, a claim that for Christians identifies him definitively as the Messiah. Thus, as we draw closer to these two characters, we do not see them diverging in their differences, but instead approaching identity. Only one feature seems to distinguish them with any certainty: Jesus Barabbas is guilty of murder,[23] whereas Jesus Christ stands accused of sedition in the eyes of Rome and blasphemy in the eyes of the Jews. Luke 23:19, incidentally, invokes the charge of sedition against Barabbas as well, reinforcing the near identity of the two figures by adding a political element to Barabbas's homicide. Both Mark and Luke call him a "rebel" who had participated in "sedition" (or an "insurection") while Matthew refers to him as "a notable prisoner" (though in John 18:40 he is identified as a "robber," perhaps to make him a less sympathetic figure by reducing him to a common criminal). Both of these two men named Jesus were associated with or accused of sedition (even if in one case the charges were trumped up) and in this their two identities converge.

Since for Holy Writ symbolic truth is vastly more important than historical veracity, we may ask whether the Jesus of double aspect (Christ-Barabbas) does not in this case represent, among other things, the complexity of the human being. He is at one and the same time a master/teacher[24] and a rebel/murderer. In fact, the moral human being holds within itself two incomplete personalities, opposite yet akin. They do not stand apart from each other as one good and the other evil (an oversimplification intended to provide an escape from the moral problem). On the contrary, the "Christ" aspect of the personality is, so to speak, "ethical" because it *reflects upon* good and evil; the "Barabbas" aspect of the personality is unreflective and hence *succumbs* to evil. As the robber in John's Gospel, he acts on impulse when he steals, yielding to the evil (equivalent to the *daimon*) within. But John's "robber" Barabbas is a vile and contemptible figure in contrast to the more glamorous "insurrectionist" Barabbas of the synoptic gospels, who must surely have had a tremendous appeal to rank-and-file Jews under the yoke of Roman oppression. Nevertheless, the insurrectionist killer is as unreflective as the common thief in succumbing to destructive inner impulses when he attempts to throw off the Roman yoke by violent means. Barabbas (the political rebel) and Christ (the spiritual savior) are both Messianic figures, but they stand at opposite ends of the Messianic spectrum: Messiah as Conquering Hero, the Lion of Judah (Gen. 49:9; Rev. 5:5), and Messiah as Suffering Servant (Is. 53). Barabbas seeks to bring about the promised Jewish kingdom through militancy and acts of violence; Christ renounces violence and promises to usher in a spiritual kingdom based on love. Thus, when Pilate makes his offer of release, the rabble is faced with a fundamental choice: What kind of Messiah do they want to deliver them?

Neither education nor restrictions *per se* constrain the mob when it is confronted with Pilate's question, "Which of these two do you want me to set free?" In unison the people cry, "Barabbas!" Symbolically speaking, this declares, "I am the 'son of' (*bar*) my father, ruthless political violence." Indeed, the cry "Barabbas!" constitutes the culminating moment of Bach's *St. Matthew Passion* of 1729. Symbolically, choosing Barabbas means releasing the killer that slumbers in each of us. This is precisely the same kind of act as that of the modern television viewer who, staring at some cultural, historical, or social debate—all eminently ethical—reaches for the remote control and switches the channel, "selecting" a so-called action movie (the verb is enclosed in quotation marks because this modern spectator, far more like his or her Colosseum counterpart than many may think, is unconscious, and leaves the choice to the internal *daimon*). The magical and hypocritical label "action movie" points to a form of entertainment whose exceptional visual quality and realism set before the modern viewer's eyes deaths that are, ironically, far more violent than those offered in the Colosseum, which had to cater to much more barbaric tastes.

Likewise, just as Greek theater and its decimated thinking public had to surrender, when confronted with the triumphal advance of the Roman circus and the crowds flocking to it, by readjusting the bleachers and the stage, so today the few means of communication that still compel reflection retreat and regroup in the face of media far more primitive, violent, and all-pervasive. Faced with this objective data, we "have no choice": there is no turning back to Greek theater, living as we do amid the roar of the Roman arena. But precisely because the actual moral earth is lost to us, moral persons today must set their feet on the sands of the arena. And the finger of the gladiator who has fallen in his own blood and is begging for his life is putting the question to us as passive spectators.

Since the symbolic sacrifice of Almachius, 1,600 years have passed. On the day of his martyrdom, as Theodoret of Cyrus[25] writes, the emperor Flavius Honorius banned gladiatorial duels throughout the empire, and the Christian revolution of love began to reshape the conscience of mankind, described by later writers as "warped wood."[26] But for a thousand years Christianity succeeded only in muzzling and containing a worsening situation, one that had been ushered in with the passage from the human dimension of the *polis* to the voracious violence of imperial society.

Over the past thousand years, movements such as the Renaissance, and later, the Enlightenment, have weakened the Christian repression of violence and the general taboo against spectacles not given ecclesiastical sanction. This was inevitable, and in many respects it was right that it came to pass. But such restored tolerance of violence comes at a price. An eternal part of human nature is making a comeback, nourished by the boundless commercialization of spectacle; we are experiencing a resurgence of the flourishing *daimon* of Theodoret and the Roman taste for blood.

The potential of the human being is neither *all* good nor *all* bad. It is both good *and* bad combined. Even so, the "Romanization" of Greek theater has already spoken for the fact that only a few years of historical and cultural change are needed for the flowering of human wickedness, whereas several millennia are not enough to teach us goodness, especially if they are attended by the virtually irreversible effects of mass civilization. Almachius settled on his long itinerary, and then attained his goal with infinite and steady patience. He was killed in a matter of seconds, by people who could neither make a decision nor construct a plan, who carried out no project, but simply erupted at the promptings of the *daimon*. This is the asymmetrical power of evil. In the arena, within seconds, the massive roar multiplies and the surge of violence accelerates. However, there exists no corresponding *daimon* of the good, capable of stirring up the masses to goodness. Almachius was alone, like every spectator in the Greek theater, with his weighty conscience.

It has been said that society, like the individual, has no wings; as for betterment, we must advance slowly, step by step. But evil sprouts wings more readily than good ever could. With the mass effect, and with technology, the eruption of demons is picking up speed. Only ethical education, like the pilgrimage made by Almachius across deserts and seas, remains personal and slow.

John Peck is a poet and Jungian analyst with a private practice in Connecticut. He received his diploma from the C. G. Jung Institute, Zürich, and is a member of the International Association for Analytical Psychology (IAAP) and the Jungian Psychoanalytic Association (JPA) of New York City. He previously taught English literature and writing at Princeton University, Mount Holyoke College, the University of Zürich, and Skidmore College. His publications include *Collected Shorter Poems 1966-1996* (Northwestern University Press, 2003) and *Red Strawberry Leaf* (University of Chicago Press, 2005). He has translated and edited two books by Luigi Zoja: *Cultivating the Soul* (2005) (with Mark Kyburz) and *Ethics and Analysis* (2007). With Sonu Shamdasani and Mark Kyburz he recently co-translated Jung's *Liber Novus* or *Red Book* (W. W. Norton/Philemon, 2009) and is currently working on other projects for the Philemon Foundation.

AFTERWORD

Zoja among Others: Between the Ego and a Hard Place

JOHN PECK

> All behaved as though they had been stained with murder, and on this day [*the day of pitchers for the new wine, the Choes festival in Athens, a* miasma hemera *or day of pollution*] all Athenians are Oresteioi .... The new wine is imbibed [at separate tables and in silence] as though it carried blood guilt.
>
> —Walter Burkert, *Homo Necans*[1]

As I begin these notes on Luigi Zoja's essays about human violence, based on lectures given between 2000 and 2008 in Texas, Brazil, the Czech Republic, Switzerland, and Italy, memory returns me to the early 1990s, when I came back to the USA after some years away. Several months before that, a stark little dream confronted me at close range with Old Glory, its regiment of white stars off-screen, its red stripes billowing across their field of snow, their slow undulations provoking nausea and underlining a plain fact—*that red means blood*—as if I needed an elementary-school primer about such facts. Yet so I did: for more than one year after my return, my sensing remained keenly alive to the potential for violence, anywhere at any time. To be sure, during those same months a shooting took place on a nearby grade-school playground, and a teacher was shot in his classroom. But specific atrocities—frequent affairs[2]—proved not to be the occasion for the constant alert I felt. Since then, accounts I have read by veterans returning from the brutal invasion and occupation of Iraq show that two features of their experience have tallied with some of Zoja's subsidiary themes—a high incidence of suicide, and variations on the theme of callous "military psychiatry."[3] In addition, these same personnel are subject to a chronic miasma that their assigned medical personnel and their own communities often leave unaddressed,[4] a condition suggesting that a strange affinity spans their inner states and my own sensing a decade earlier: the tight little god of hypervigilance has attended us both. Had I remembered Euripides and Callimachus, however—Burkert's sources for those sentences from his study of ritual murder in archaic Greece—I might also have asked myself about the adaptive function at work in such keen sensing. For, beyond initiating a return to my home place, the objective psyche dispassionately used that tribal symbol to mark my kinship with fellow murderers, and theirs with me. Like a smoker trying to break the habit by wearing a nicotine patch, I received an appliqué cut from the tribal fabric.[5] And so, like Orestes the mother-killer, I was journeying home and feeling myself apart, though apart in sharpened belonging.

A veteran—Latin *uetus*, "old," and *ueteranus*—denotes someone rightly aged by combat but also a retired official rich in experience. With the harvest of "old" experience from the Vietnam catastrophe swiftly trashed by U.S. officials, the country now joins those few modern states that have invaded crushingly without warrant: Italy, Germany, and the Soviet Union. Both Luigi Zoja and Anthony Stevens attend closely to the scandals of honor and guilt piled on the donkey *uetus* by the criminal *ueteranus*: a consummate fraud propelled by flimsy archetypal projections leaves soldiers to shoulder deranging moral burdens alone.[6]

A Copernican revolution in the de-centering of the human ego—first by the lonely Polish mathematician who levered himself off the earth for a look around, then by a code-breaking Viennese doctor, then by a visionary Swiss alienist, and finished off, as Zoja has argued in *Cultivating the Soul* (2005), by archetypalist James Hillman[7]—has mounted an epochal *Putsch* against ordinary species hubris. Luigi Zoja has tracked certain consequences of this overthrow in his several books, particularly in *Growth and Guilt: Psychology and the Limits of Development* (1995).

From a Venetian family that migrated to Milan for employment, Zoja was born there in 1943 (although outside the city, which was then under bombardment). During the student unrest of the late '60s he studied economics and the new discipline of sociology, turning directly from these to Jung's psychology. Zoja is a past president of both the Centro Italiano di Psicologia Analitica and the International Association of Analytical Psychology, and the Chair of the IAAP's Ethics Committee. He shifted his practice to New York City during the several years that bracketed the 2001 attacks, and returned to practice in Milan, where he now devotes most of his time to writing on themes that probe the contemporary ego's perch—Western European, and North and South American—on its shaken ground. Works in progress include *The Death of the Neighbor* and *Ajax's Folly: Paranoia, Society, and History*.

Consequently, the audience for Zoja's work is both Italian and Anglo-American. After the September 11 attacks and while still in New York, he edited, with colleague Donald Williams, *Jungian Reflections on September 11* (2002), whose Italian edition (*L'incubo globale*, 2002) includes a bonus essay by playwright Roberto Buffagni.[8] In formal terms, the most innovative essay on the theme of violence by any Jungian writer to date can be found there: "The Terror and the Temple" by São Paulo analyst Victor-Pierre Stirnimann (also the translator of Chapter 2 in this volume, on the Aztec decline). In his long "Transatlantic Reflections," in the *September 11* anthology, Zoja turns over the related questions of hatred for the USA and its own psychic vulnerability on the receiving end of nemesis. His virtue as a European is not only the compliment he has paid us by living here, but also his different perspective compared to that of many European observers.[9]

That is, in his view the historian's genetic scrutiny of documented, blatant occasions of blowback, needful as such scrutiny may be, stops short of full responsibility. A psychological view instead insists that "nemesis can surface wherever there is a corresponding psychological constellation."[10] That way of putting it illuminates nicely my returnee's hypervigilance to North American violence. Zoja draws the corollary inference that, should the USA find ways of converting its arrogance into humility, then it might move toward a new psychological attitude. In view for him here is not the workings of politics so much as the thrust, far beneath them, of what might grow out of "a political psychology," as he had already advocated in *Growth and Guilt*.[11] Such a psychology, like a folktale's treasure-hard-to-attain, penetrates to the nuclei of reigning attitudes:

> The political options of the global *pólis* also demand, now perhaps for the very first time, the payment of a clear psychological price .... The problem of the limits of growth assumes its truest guise and presents itself as a limitation of human expectations .... This *cul-de-sac*, though apparently created by the age of modern technology, gives the Greeks a new pertinence, [for in myth, tragedy, and philosophy they inscribed limits] onto the single table of their law.[12]

Political psychology, then, colonizes a de-centering of the human ego. As Zoja's Introduction to this volume declares, psychology can study nothing more important than human destructiveness, because it is innate or structural, and because it can be remedied only by patient individual labor.

As astute as are Roberto Buffagni's reflections on prophetic Melville and John Mason's Puritan liquidation of the Pequot natives of Connecticut, which parallel Susan Falludi's attempts to run masculine American violence to ground in the earliest Indian wars (*The Terror Dream*, 2007),[13] such readings proceed straight from the outside in. Falludi simply presents one of her own dreams as an advance poster for the outer situation. As attractive as such readings can seem—for example, German journalist Charlotte Beradt's contemporary reflections on the material she gathered in the *Third Reich of Dreams*[14]—they are no substitute for depth psychology's path from the inside out, which radically supplements the ego standpoint and deflates ego hubris, its enterprises since birth.

Zoja's address to American collective psychology is particularly Greek. In his first essay here he likens it to the psychology of Odysseus. And the shadow brother for wily, multiplex, vagabond loner Odysseus, as Sophocles painted him in *Ajax*, is the ox-like, rolling, steadfastly indomitable fighter whose heroism and honor are fatally simplistic: the John Wayne of the Trojan War, whose fatal boast is that he will fight his way to glory or *kleos* without the help of the gods. Zoja observes in his first chapter that the USA's penchant for reliance on overwhelming military force, alongside our economic gigantism and habitual trespass of limits, almost guarantees that the nemesis in our case will be "pollution by force."

Thus Ajax, a kind of archaic Paul Bunyan turned George Patton, slaughters penned-up cattle thinking they are the encamped Greeks who deprived him of Achilles' armor. In shame Ajax kills himself.

Deranged by the *menis* or anger of the gods, he reaps blowback from the powers that he had declared supernumerary (in American terms, consuming the nation's wealth in militarism while contaminating its own personnel with depleted-uranium ammunition). Homer's Odysseus, as Zoja observes, swings between mind and heart, calculation and emotion, *phrena* and *thumon*; but in his flexible duality there works a certain conscious sanity. Sophocles' chorus in *Ajax* warns: bypass limit or *peiras*, losing that *sophronos* or sound mind that the powers love, and *thumos menis* or fatefully blind wrath will consume you from the inside out. Ajax has conflated honor with hubris, turning the simply noble into the unlimited.

This theme, a polluting force blowing back on hubris, of course transcends the American instance. Zoja's third chapter in this book, on honor and the duel, treats something far more flexible: those ritual, animally-rooted limits to destructiveness, though mere vestiges now, which still mark precious containments of instinctive aggression. The mental fog in which such aggression rules nations is summarized by Daniel Ellsberg (releaser of the Pentagon Papers in the Vietnam era, who catalyzed the end of the Nixon regime), who repeatedly demonstrates that whether in Vietnam or Iraq, "an awful lot of people have died because a few people have been afraid to be called names."[15] Such is the false honor for which the honorable duel supplies perhaps the only archetypal antidote, in Zoja's reading. Neither the Jungian analyst and evolutionary psychiatrist Anthony Stevens in *The Roots of War and Terror* (2004) nor the ethologist Eibl-Eibesfeldt in his magisterial *Biology of Peace and War* from the 1970s discusses dueling, though both attend closely to ritualized conflict. Zoja's essays here are based on exploratory lectures, which have permitted him, in this case as in his essay on nightmares, to reconnoiter new territory.

Allowing for differences in genre and aim, I have found it useful to set Zoja's work alongside prose by Italians that I read in my twenties and thirties, by Nicola Chiaromonte and Elémire Zolla, and by American-born Iris Origo.[16] The navigation by these writers of two cultures, Italy's and America's during and after World War II, took stock of an emerging mass civilization in terms that still animate Zoja's writing, terms quite other than those in Walter Benjamin's ambitious critique (by way of a materialist history threaded with messianic theology). Yet Jung's perspective extends further, both downwards and upwards, than Benjamin's. In the Socratic spirit of Gaetano Salvemini,[17] the historian briefly imprisoned and then self-exiled to England and the USA in 1925, I pose myself this question about Jung and the others surveyed here: "The archetype, natural and implacable, utterly revises our historical and political categories—that is what you *want* to say, isn't it?" Although his followers seldom add directly to Jung's central reflections on human violence, what they bring makes little sense without those reflections. Alongside Zoja I include Marie-Louise von Franz, Joseph Henderson, James Hillman, John Weir Perry, John Dourley, Wolfgang Giegerich, Graham Saayman, Anthony Stevens, and Donald Kalsched.

In Zoja's widely ranging study of *The Father* (2001),[18] Chapter 15 on "The Disenchantment of War" distills themes shared among historians, Stevens and other Jungians, and the ethologists, within the framework of his country's experience. Italian society today "follows the general path of the Western world, and especially the United States, with a certain delay; but at the beginning of the twentieth century it pioneered a number of phenomena," namely, mass mobilization; sporadic and futile mutiny against slaughter; fragging and mass desertions; the disintegration of heroism, authority, and the father's status; and regression to herd archetypes. From Russia's revolution to Italy's pioneer dictatorship, a seeming age before Vietnam, the modern world was forged by this corrosive disillusionment with the warrior father and, through unconscious transmission, with the patriarchal family. The historian George Mosse has treated the same disillusionment with the fathers in Weimar and early Nazi Gemany.[19] One motive for Zoja's depth study of fathering, from antiquity until now, is the invented character of that pivotal role. The first several chapters in *The Father* keep ethology firmly in view; fatherhood "implies a radical and permanent departure from the norms of purely animal life,"[20] arranging quite a new social order, which now breaks open and cracks up in mass civilization. Like Joseph Henderson, Zoja studies both initiation and the cultural unconscious (the latter term coming from Henderson) in order to bring Jung's work to bear upon modern situations in perennial cultural terms—such as the ritual tribal passage into the constructed world of the fathers where men find their way "between the clashing rocks of achievement and folly."[21] Anthony Stevens maintains that initiation is human culture's only decisive check on the homicidal archetypal aggression of men.[22]

This precarious factor and its epic Greek prototype affected Zoja's own family of origin. At the outset of Chapter 15 of *The Father*, he writes, "like Ulysses's son, my father had just been born when his father departed for the Great War."[23] When Zoja's grandfather at last returned and sat down at table in uniform, Zoja's father, still a boy, excited and importunate, was banished by that patriarch to the kitchen. "Who is that man?" he cried to the kitchen maids through his tears. In "Individuation and Paideia" (1997), Zoja devotes a key section to Telemachus, where one finds the mythic profile for the episode with Zoja's father.[24] Odysseus's son faces a civilizational task *par excellence.* Zoja argues that analysis in Jung's spirit addresses this task meaningfully where the family and the state no longer can. That is, such analysis can serve us as *paideia* once served post-Homeric Greece, as cultural formation attentive to the *archai.* Before Odysseus returns to Ithaca Telemachus seeks "my father's fame" from Nestor and Mentes. What he seeks, in colloquy with that interior ego ideal "capable of shoring up his own" and pushing it further, is his only way of emerging, properly initiated, from the clouds of maternal influence. With both Jung and the ethologists we can add that the same quest engages an archetypal release-mechanism, the imprinting of mature manhood upon a surrogate identity. When the living father in fact returns, Telemachus is inwardly prepared to step his bow with its lethal string.

Just behind Homer's narrative, then, and likewise behind Zoja's family story in line with modern Italy's pioneer disintegration of paternal authority, stands the charged finding reported by both Anthony Stevens and Eibl-Eibesfeldt: namely, that the civilization we know has grown stronger through time, *not in spite of but chiefly because of strife and warfare,* out of masculinity's competitive and destructive bio-psychic root: *Strife the all-father,* as Heraclitus said in convening the endless seminar on conflict. Therefore, there is no other way through war and human murderousness than through this archetypal thicket of dynamic predispositions to violent action. Even that brave innovation in peace action, Gandhi and Khan Abdul Khan's practice of *satyagraha,* takes aggression as its high-octane fuel.

At the same time, we live during the most precarious of eras for masculine archetypal qualities and their social incarnations, during which the age-old habit of *reinforcing identity* through both aggression and reductivism—Zoja's interlocking themes, next to Jung's keystone themes of identification, archaic identity, and dissociation—abides unbroken. *Hic Rhodos, hic salta!* And the waters one leaps at Rhodes are those of Zoja's sketch of ego formation, in constriction around paranoid attack, in "Nightmares." There the findings of ethology bear down heavily. His description there of ego-genesis in our species is explicitly tragic: the paranoid projection of death's terror, along with fear of the other, arise as soon as "I" stands separate and visible to itself. Ego-genesis midwifes the false perception that our own kind is alien ("pseudo-speciation")—a tragic illusion to be dispelled; and Greek tragedy gives Zoja his main analogy for the cultural role played by analysis. Plato often alluded to contemporary Greek tragedy in his dialogues; Claudia Barrachi's study of the *Republic* concludes that for Plato, too, the city-state, which for Socrates makes the psyche dynamically visible,[25] is at war with its opposite number but also

> is at war with itself at the same time, precisely in asserting itself as self-same .... In both cases, at stake is the destruction of the other .... This city results from a dream of *phusis* (of a natural ground [for peace and justice]). Yet at the heart of this dream is the vision, however exorcised and projected, of horror and destruction, of difference so unsustainable as to require enmity .... In the repression and projection of such deep disquietudes for the sake of order and stillness lies the disorder, the utter injustice, of this dream—therefore, a nightmare.[26]

Zoja's "Nightmares" reads our collective chances in light of the watershed era of World War I, with Italy's pioneer episode close at hand. Zoja's discreet summary of his patient Martin, a former Wehrmacht trooper whose suicide long after World War II moves Zoja to rhyme his fate with Primo Levi's, might be that of a Telemachus deprived of the chance for adequate release into the warrior-father's honor and adequacy. The receding zone of the older Mars still exerts, through our bio-psychic ground, its driving claims; and so, they might have us ask, did Martin turn self-wounding because of a mother complex, survivor's guilt, and the atrocious conditions of mechanized killing? Zoja tactfully supplies insight into the structure of Martin's nightmare while leaving us to our own inferences. That nightmare repeated itself because in our conditions the solution remains out of reach. The occasion of Martin's self-murder calls up all the *archai* of destructiveness and poises them along the rim of history, modern ruptures of masculinity, and the deep cross-lighting of crevasses in animal-human ethology, but it properly challenges any neat personal summaries.

Throughout Zoja's essays here, as in his earlier books, runs the urgent motive to see through the present and the recent past to the workings of those bio-psychic *archai*, not in their invisible transcendence but in their varied effects. Long before Cormac McCarthy, Joseph Conrad epitomized such urgency by recommending: "In the dangerous element immerse." The same motive erupted into Jung's Dionysian descent during World War I, and shaped his later sense of the mass situation that morphs around us now at greater speed and fiercer risk.

The long-term working of archetypes, not surprisingly in Jung's thought, burrows into evolution. Zoja, among other writers inspired by Jung, each drenched from immersion in the meaning of human creativity and destructiveness, echoes the tensions long active within evolutionary thinking about aggression and mass murder. Paul Crook's survey of Darwinian thought up through sociobiology, in the light of its cultural reception, makes it clear that from Jung and von Franz to Wolfgang Giegerich and Zoja, the ethological view in Lorenz and Eibl-Eibesfeldt prevails strongly over peace biology's holdout view, in which Darwinian terms—war as no longer adaptive, "an evolutionary anachronism"[27]—push back feebly against ethology's respect for innate or archetypal destructiveness. Giegerich's killer-human, together with his analysis of Christian civilization's explosive destructiveness,[28] and Zoja's grounding of that view in ego-genesis as tragically paranoid and destructive, in "Nightmares," accord in large part with Lorenz and Eibl-Eibesfeldt (though definitely not with Social Darwinism: see Chapter 5, "Reductivism"). Jungian psychologist Graham Saayman's work with the African baboon, bottlenose dolphin, and whales, as well as with human families, works non-traumatic territory without relaxing ethology's discipline.[29]

Yet even ethologists, archetypal by disposition, disappoint von Franz in her "Transformed Berserk" of the mid-1980s, where only the long-suffered attendance upon archetypal wrath (exemplified in the Swiss captain and judge Nicklaus von Flüe's visions at 45) points the way. In Klaus's vision of a Wotanic wanderer wearing bearskin that shines with a sword's reflected gleams, the shamanic figure's whole aspect fills with an eros "like honey." Klaus's Christian god-image has been filled out by the Germanic god of war, healing, and vision. The case that von Franz makes, guided by Jung, supplies a transformed and newly effectual separateness that, as we are prepared to see, crucially countervails the tragically separated archaic ego in Zoja's essay on nightmares:

> We cannot integrate such divine powers of aggression in our ordinary selves. All that hopeful benevolent talk about integrating one's aggression is nonsense. We can only, through our efforts and suffering, bring forth an integration of these forces within the Self. . . . Modern zoologists like Konrad Lorenz and innumerable psychologists write today about the problem of aggression and how to integrate, abreact, or suppress it. Brother Klaus's vision shows us how he *really* succeeded in integrating and transforming it. Then it is no longer what we call aggression but rather a clearly defined separateness and firmness of the individual which succeeds in remaining steadfastly in "himself" and does not succumb to group or mass suggestions. . . . This is still clearly a very remote goal for humanity and in the meantime nations and groups will inevitably go on fighting each other.[30]

Graham Saayman would be the first to appreciate the timing of Jung's kundalini seminar and its crucial animal symbolism, coeval with Jung's 1933 essay on Brother Klaus. The war god and the god of love, the bear that rages and the honey-seeking bear, enact a yoga of integration.

I shall return to Zoja after setting both Stevens and Kalsched in the light of von Franz on Brother Klaus. Her estimate here, aimed at a woefully minimal development of eros by the human species, marks the *peiras* or limit, and also the *telos* or goal, of both individuation and intergroup/intra-group psychology (to borrow Stevens's ethological terms) in Jung himself. Here and no further!—yet we haven't even begun to get there. The impressive thing about Stevens's firmly ethological summary in *The Roots of War* (1989) is that between its argument and Donald Kalsched's review of it, the full tension within Jung's work around human destructiveness becomes explicit. Stevens borrows Kalsched's Epimetheus as a myth to characterize Stevens's own diagnosis of collective denial about the drastic facts of our self-created emergency. Kalsched, while acknowledging the potency of Stevens's summary, sees it backtracking to the rationalism it would leave behind, slipping into "archetypal determinism" and abandoning Jung's depth: "The psyche, that indeterminate 'third' which was Jung's primary preoccupation, drops out."[31] Nonetheless, near the end of his argument Stevens sounds very like von Franz, after he cites Jung's commentary on *The Secret of the Golden Flower* (on the non-rational solutions won through alert suffering): "One has to endure them in full consciousness until something radical shifts inside or outside which leads to their transcendence."[32]

Regardless of how one assesses the dialogue between Stevens and Kalsched, it discloses a sustained debate over the fate of Jung's notions of identification, archaic identity, and dissociation versus the "compendious personality" that was his goal (his phrase in "Transformation Symbolism in the Mass," composed in 1941while on tactical retreat during an invasion scare). John Dourley's long meditation on this debate in 2003, "Archetypal Hatred as Social Bond: Strategies for Its Dissolution," gives the best review to date of Jung's developing social psychology, which "though so apparently fragile, is in a position to make a substantial contribution to any theory that would seek first principles for the survival of the species." Like von Franz and Jung, Dourley brackets off all well-meaning political and economic measures as lesser psychological solutions that only "delay rather than undermine the next archetypal disaster." Turning to Samuel Huntington's clash of civilizations, Zoja's subject in his penultimate chapter here, Dourley steers away from dead-end post-Enlightenment rationalism and determinism (Kalsched's concern in his review of Stevens earlier) to Jung's transconscious psyche and its irrational basis in the need for human beings to redeem crushing and amoral divine factors, as did Job: "Unless a sense of the common, deeply human origin of cultural archetypal differences becomes the centerpiece of a new myth ..., Huntington's paradigm of an ongoing clash of civilizations would appear to carry the day and to define our future."[33] While neither Dourley now, nor von Franz then, cited John Weir Perry, it was Perry's last book in the late '80s that already sketched such an emerging cultural myth, from roots in the death-rebirth cycles of psychosis and myths of the royal father: *The Heart of History: Individuality in Evolution.* The line that it marks in the sand reaches back to the Pharaohs and out into the future. The *homo totus* of Gerhard Dorn's alchemy and Jung's individuation process proves to be no private matter but a critically makeweight effort in the greater balance of things.

In a pointed way, Jung's own Dionysian descent in 1913-1921 begins with a plunge into the animal psyche—the realm of the dead as a lost realm of instinct—which plays out in Jung's aim at the alchemical *homo totus.* In Chapter 6 of this book Zoja echoes James Hillman's distinction between culture, which flowers, and civilization, which works.[34] Originally this distinction was Nietzsche's;[35] both inventions, of course, distinguish the human/animal species. Anthony Stevens quotes from an interview of Jung's in which Jung says that Western civilization has dissociated us from our base: "We forget that we are still primates."[36] Already in the 1980s, and again in 2002, Hillman addressed the American experiment and psyche by focusing correctively on the *animal* soul.[37] His intuition amplifies Jung's remark to Swiss geographer Hans Carol in 1950: "We forget that we are still primates—that we must therefore take account of these primitive levels of our soul. ... Through our civilizing potentialities we have gotten off on a wrong track."[38]

Zoja's ethical concerns throughout serve this same instinctual-spiritual entirety that was Jung's main offering. Zoja's touchstones make of responsibility a rich task, not a ruled page. The trick is to acknowledge sharp limits while sustaining ambivalence, the complexity of ethical gray zones, and the maturing in them that Neumann called "ethical personalization" (Primo Levi, and Zoja's remarkable relationship with an informer-patient, illustrate these in *Ethics and Analysis*[39]). The trick is also to accommodate those long stretches of time that dissolve ego flight and impatience and permit guilt's time-release to deepen us (Traudl Junge, Hitler's secretary, in Chapter 1 of this book). The view opened up by Zoja's political psychology begins, then, with the young human's primate brain, which in a single day absorbs as much stimulation as people in traditional societies receive in one year, and goes on to recapitulate the trauma of archaic ego-genesis and its kinship with nightmare (Chapter 4). A political psychology, therefore, also positions itself between Erich Neumann's child and analyst Neil Micklem's "intolerable image" in order to slow down conventional ethics sufficiently to expand the human animal's chances for ethical density.

Zoja does not turn us toward Hillman on Roscher's classic treatment of nightmares and instinct,[40] perhaps because nature as Pan, the ambivalent image of desire/fear that heals civilized splitting, glances off our heaped wreckage. That is, this civilization forestalls nature with something drastic—reductive, functionalistic, traumatic—that frustrates the psychic *coniunctio* and discards its fruits, whether they be the honorable duel that confines destructiveness, or the tragic enactment that extracts luminosity from paranoid splitting and violence. Hillman's own meditation on human destructiveness, *A Terrible Love of War*, which leaves out ethology's long-term view of the roots of aggression, and rules out the bio-psychic take on alien otherness, also momentarily surrenders when confronted with the paradoxical lamb of the Christian Apocalypse, assimilating it to the psychotic incubus and dragon seeds of violence rife in Western religion. And so, for an instant, Hillman does not see it for the uniting symbol that it is: the wrathful lamb, lamb turned cataclysmic ram, which primordially *completes* the Christian god-image by reinstating Yahweh Lord of Hosts.[41] This composite, the wrathful lamb, is the prototype for Klaus's mysticism. Such rare moments of reduced dimensionality in Hillman's work demonstrate how difficult it is actually to grasp, and go on holding, what the original nightmare of ego-genesis in Zoja's reading scans. Its fissions are what the primordial uniting symbols gather home. The human ego, however ably it accommodates the non-ego trammels of instinct and spirit, remains up against the hard place of limit *and* transformation, a paradoxical hardness that our bewildering birthright declares can also, with the endurance seen in Brother Klaus by Jung and von Franz, turn into honey.

Jung perceived the archetype nearly in quantum terms: a self-presenting image in one vein, and in the other a dynamic pattern waiting to go into action. Zoja's place among this array of writers hinges on his feeling for the ways in which the action-half of archetypal polarity affects civic and social life. In action, whether civic and real or tragic and staged, the old Greeks declared the soul to be at last visible. Zoja finds all of these dimensions gathered into the analytic process, which carries the luminosity of meaning that recent history has darkened. An action, in Greek, is *drama*. Tragic drama, which need not end in calamity—Euripides' *Alcestis*, for example—is enactment that forces responsible decision or *proairesis*, compels conscious action amid conflict, invokes the divine, and breathes the ozone of heroic confusion and fate. Eric Voegelin said of 5th-century Athenian tragedy what Jung said of his own personal *katabasis* in 1913-1921: that it was a Dionysian descent into the divine depth of *psukhē*, against the backdrop of strife construed as the very order of the world.[42] It also prompted Aristotle to apply the new diagnostic practice of Hippocrates to tragedy's emotions, *krisis*, and unfolding, as the parallel courses run by illness, cure, and insight.[43] It is but one step from such large integrations to depth psychology's reliance on tragic drama for themes in Freud and for the shape of dream action in Jung. Likewise, it is one more step from Socrates' definition of courage in the *Laches* as a deep knowledge of good *and* evil, to Jung on the morality of evil and Zoja's meditations on Neumann's new ethic, Primo Levi's gray zone, and the seasoning of responsibility by time, guilt, and ethical complexity. When tragedy turns into a question of literary register or social critique only, its primordial function has slipped from view. The ethical themes that inexorably expand into action compelling full witness, and that take the good-*and*-evil of the *Laches* into performance, splice darkness and light; in them the relative visibility of the whole psyche moves drastically toward meaning.

Five of Zoja's essays in *Cultivating the Soul* (2005) take up this durable invention, one of them explicitly linking tragic meaning to the fruit of the analytic process.[44] A long sixth essay in the same book deals with Greek *paideia*, a matter more inclusive than our "education." In *Ethics and Analysis* Zoja reflects at several points on tragic enactment and narration as the great lost rituals of meaning in the West, supplanted by meager surrogates.[45] In a word, tragic narration provides Zoja with the best *cultural* antecedent for what analysis secures when it gives the modern person a supplemental *paideia*. Tragic narrative supplies to his recent essays on violence a pervasive background, but also a pivotal accent, the first for the human ego's god-almightiness, and the second for that same ego's birth in paranoid fright.

In "The *Agamemnon* and the Contemporary Presence of Tragedy," Zoja ties the modern concern with tragedy to its testing of hubris and limits, the richness of ambivalence, and its shredding of rationalism, the progress myth, and monochromatic ethics.[46] This modern concern is individual, however: a hell-bent civilization avoids meanings that only single persons can work out responsibly over time. *By Hercules!* as the old Latins proclaimed in the open air, for this solitary labor is not selfish, because its honesty and sweat countervail the sophisms at work in history.

I suspect that Zoja's attention to action-as-image, or the whole archetype seen through its dynamic aspect, frames his reading of the archetypal push from nature to act responsibly—a paradoxical push, since we have seized godlike powers while staying in a fog of denial. Thus, Kalsched's Prometheus-Epimetheus myth accurately gets our situation, as acknowledged by Stevens. By staying with tragic action and its enforced demands for action and insight, Zoja stays just to one side of Stevens's focus upon bio-psychic determinants, closer to Kalsched's attention to trauma (see Zoja's chapter on the Aztec decline in this volume). The psyche's mixed responses to trauma and calamity remain partly open for Kalsched; the trauma defenses, rigidly conservative and monstrous though protective, lock up the creative potentials that ego sacrifice can pry loose.[47] My guess is that Kalsched's inner demonic protector stands as the psychic cousin to Zoja's traumatized original ego, shocked and paranoid upon emergence into separateness, which evolves only by generalizing its aggressive function into murderous repetition, the dragon's teeth of massacre and war. Ethology's account approaches the Teutonic myths of world destruction; pseudo-speciation, which falsely converts one's own kind into a mortal threat, finally collapses into Ragnarok and the *Götterdämmerung* (Zoja touches on the uniquely suicidal theology of the Germanic gods in *Cultivating the Soul*). Either situation, whether Kalsched's abuse zone or Zoja's nightmare warp, forms a crucible for tragic myths, which in current circumstances tend toward either extinction or transformation.

Therefore, a moving three-way colloquy has been developing among Stevens, Kalsched, and Zoja over a twenty-year span, with von Franz and Jung as their sponsors. Kalsched turns to the victim, attends to traumatic non-ego defenses, and invokes the myth, borrowed by Stevens, that mates fatal technical precocity with denial, in Prometheus and Epimetheus. Stevens borrows his myth from Kalsched because, from here on out, even ego defenses may prove to be species-fatal (they surround the human ego to shield it from whatever would disturb it too much, to reduce good old Paleolithic danger and chanciness to a workable minimum). Zoja's myth is still forming; his focus on ego-genesis in "Nightmares," in tandem with paranoid attack, positions him to read our own time as a potentially fatal phase-shift that might twist the necessary sacrifice toward evasion and conflict (the archaic shift from hunting to agriculture was not botched in that way, during the Cain/Abel transition). Whereas Stevens's human being cries, "Let me alone, don't disturb me!" Zoja's yells, "Let me at him!" Zoja's shaken human animal does so in the terror-fear of death, swiftly projected; in the simultaneous terrors of isolation and confrontation on emerging from archaic identity; and into hubris, as the drug for both kinds of terror. Not Cain but Ajax, therefore, captures one part of the mythic profile (Prometheus reduced to the archaic hunk-hero): the technique of a demigod in the body and brain of a big primate who perseverates in doing what he does best—a too-simple, steadfastly bashing honor that reinforces identity past the limit.

Nonetheless, the bony evidence for this strict acknowledgement of species hubris and denial, a smashed Late-Paleolithic skull cradling bitter knowledge, has been delivered by the excavator's trowel—even Teilhard's, a decorated stretcher-bearer in World War I and desert paleontologist. Zoja on nightmares writes a coda to Jung's long meditation on separations from herd consciousness, Lévy-Bruhl's *participation mystique*. That precious inflection into individual consciousness turns out to be, in Jung's pharmacopia, the homeopathic remedy for its dark cousin posted at human origins, the archaic lunge out of herd identity into terror. Cued initially by alarming visions, Jung's own pivotal phase, which germinated most of his life's work, was birthed by Europe's first descent into mass slaughter. His later work, mostly after the Bomb, pressed to their ethical, psychoid, and synchronisitc limits the terms of the animal-and-spirit integration that the active imaginations in his *Liber Novus* or Red Book already had stipulated as the great task. A letter from 1945 about Brother Klaus and his vision of the bear-shirted Wotanic wanderer put it this way, anticipating the later remark to Hans Carol: "The man charged with *mana*, or numinous man, has theriomorphic attributes, since he surpasses the ordinary man not only upwards but downwards."[48] The Eastern icons of Christ's baptism encode the same axis, from plunging firebird down through slimed mollusk, eel, and fish.

Greek tragic enactment descended to depth in broad daylight, like its sharp-edged cradle, the city-state, rendering the soul visible. Or so Socrates suggests in the *Republic*, in whose opening pages he is figuratively taken prisoner of war. Aeschylus's tomb mentions not his art but his service at Marathon; Sophocles was one of ten officers commanding the Athenian armed forces. *Uetus* and *ueteranus*, the old hands indeed: Do we finger these facts like collectors, or read them with the cold-hot gaze of our bio-psychic *archai*, which if left untended might render us invisible in some paroxysm? A descent assuredly beckons; but beware the *imitatio Graeca*, for a growth downwards must be one's own growth. The form taken by Zoja's myth therefore matters less than its morale, for tragic narration as a dynamic pattern welcomes all load-bearing carriers of limit, including the "numinous man."

Brother Klaus lived as a 15th-century Swiss *uetus* captain and *ueteranus* district judge, a pious paterfamilias heartsick over discord and corruption. His berserk or bear-shirt vision did not make this plain-spoken man more eloquent; his mediation saved the divided Swiss cantons from civil war, assuring national survival to the Swiss, not because of maxims but through *mana*. One thinks of toothless Gandhi in his dhoti. And such inner events, which complete a god-image and weld opposites with honey, gave evidence to Jung, in another letter thirteen years after the first use of the atomic weapon, that manifestly historical events are not the decisive ones. The ghost standing at the banquet is not noble Banquo's but Tamerlane's. To his correspondent Jung developed the Brother Klaus *novum* without naming it, noting the presumptive existence "of a supreme being *who is in the main unconscious*" and at the same time drives "an impelling force" that wants "wider consciousness and responsibility" from our wet clay ("and man has not even begun yet to know himself").

History? Neither Terry Eagleton on tragedy nor even Walter Benjamin's signal "Critique of Violence"[49] can lend me, as a returnee to blood-striped Domination Central, the megawatt glimpse into Klaus's objective transformation. Colonnus echoes there, as does the flaming, commissioning bush of wrath on Sinai. The effect on Klaus of his vision renders visible those extremes within us that may meet, not endlessly clash, to immunize us against inner magma, outer miasma, and nemesis. History? "The real history of the world seems to be the progressive incarnation of the deity."[50]

Notes

INTRODUCTION

1. Bairoc reminds us that all the wars of the 19th century caused around 5½ million deaths, while in the 20th century the deaths attributed to the two World Wars alone amount to between 14 and 16 million for the First and between 37 and 44 million for the Second. By 1945, therefore, the increase in the death rate from war, during the first half of the century as compared to the previous century, comes to 1000%. See Paul Bairoc, *Victoires et déboires: Histoire économique et sociale du monde du XVI siècle a nos jours* Vol. III (Paris: Gallimard, 1997), ch. xxiv. The numbers, however, continue to be revised upwards. According to Ferguson, who includes massacres within national borders, the Soviet Gulag, and major shifts in population, the Second World War claimed between 58 and 59 million victims, while for the whole of the century the highest estimates have reached the astounding number of between 167 to 188 million. See the appendix to Niall Ferguson, *The War of the World: History's Age of Hatred* (London: Penguin, 2006). The number of people killed by others in the 20th century would be between 30 and 40 times greater than that of the 19th century. One cannot avoid acknowledging that violence has approached its absolute limit, for if the 21st century were to maintain the same rate of increase, *the human species would exterminate itself.*
2. In this book, see Chapter Two, "Trauma and Abuse: The Development of a Cultural Complex in the History of Latin America."
3. See the following: Tzvetan Todorov, *The Conquest of America: The Question of the Other*, trans. Richard Howard (Norman, OK: University of Oklahoma Press, 1999 [Seuil, Paris 1982]); David E. Stannard, *American Holocaust: The Conquest of the New World* (New York and Oxford: Oxford University Press, 1992); Samantha Power, *A Problem from Hell: America and the Age of Genocide* (New York: Basic Books, 2002); Ben Kiernan, *Blood and Soil: A World History of Genocide and Extermination, from Sparta to Darfur* (New Haven, CT: Yale University Press, 2007).

CHAPTER ONE—VIOLENT HEARTS: AMERICA'S DIVIDED SOUL

1. One of the most famous and best-studied examples is that of Cortes's victory over the vast Aztec empire. Cortes, seeking to capture Montezuma, put himself in the other man's place, whereas the Aztec emperor, terrified of confrontation mostly for psychological reasons, tried in every way to evade him. I have reconstructed this encounter in my next chapter here, "Trauma and Abuse: The Development of a Cultural Complex in the History of Latin America" (first published in T. Singer and S. L. Kimbles, eds., *The Cultural Complex: Contemporary Jungian Perspectives on Psyche and Society* [New York: Brunner-Routledge, 2004]).
2. Luigi Zoja, "Analysis and Tragedy," in *Cultivating the Soul,* trans. John Peck and Mark Kyburz (London: Free Association, 2005).
3. Bruno Snell, "Introduction," in *The Discovery of the Mind: The Greek Origins of European Thought,* trans. T. G. Rosenmeyer (Hamburg, 1946; Cambridge, MA: Harvard University Press, 1953).
4. Jacqueline de Romilly, *"Patience, mon coeur!"* (Paris: Les belles lettres, 1991).
5. *Atlantic Monthly* commissioned the *nouveau philosophe* Bernard-Henri Lévy to follow Tocqueville's travels through the USA. Lévy describes his encounter with archetypal American philosophy in the words of a police officer who stopped while Lévy was relieving himself beside a superhighway. He did not say "That's illegal" or even "You can't stop your car here," but ordered him to "Keep moving!"
6. Alexis de Tocqueville, *Democracy in America* (1835), Part II, Chapter VIII.52: "How equality leads Americans to the idea of infinite human perfectibility."
7. Today's American CEO earns around 475 times as much as the average employee, but the differential is much greater if one takes into account the value of the stock holdings that make up part of his or her remuneration. In France the differential is a mere 15 times. In 1980, an American CEO earned 40 times more than the average employee, and the difference in Europe was much less. See T. R. Reid, *The United States of Europe: The New Superpower and the End of American Supremacy* (New York: Penguin, 2005).
8. Imprisoned Americans number around two million. As a percentage of the total population, this amounts to eight times the percentage in Europe.
9. See, for example, Richard Waswo, *The Founding Legend of Western Civilization: From Virgil to Vietnam* (Hanover, NH: Wesleyan University Press; University Press of New England, 1997), and of course the famous 1944 lecture by T. S. Eliot, *What Is a Classic?* (London: Faber & Faber, 1946).
10. *Annuit Coeptis* [he has favored (our) undertakings] is the affirmative version of the Trojan prayer to Jupiter in the *Aeneid* (9.625): *Iuppiter omnipotes audacibus annue coeptis* [almighty Jupiter, favor (our) daring undertakings]. *Novus ordo s[a]ec[u]lorum* comes from the Fourth Eclogue of Virgil, where,

significantly, one finds a prefiguring of Christianity (the omission of the *a* and the *u*, philologically debatable, has opened the door to magical numerology: the letters number 13, in line with the original number of states). *E[x] pluribus unum*, spelled that way in Jefferson's contribution to the early design, and likely derived from the motto of London's *Gentleman's Magazine*, spelled in the same way, furnishes one more bridge, like the *Confessions* of Saint Augustine, between pagan Rome and Christianity (omission of the *x* again produces 13 letters).

11. Charles Gibson, *Spain in America* (New York: Harper & Row, 1966), and Gibson, ed., *The Spanish Tradition in America* (New York: Harper & Row, 1968).
12. See John Ellis, *Brute Force: Allied Strategy and Tactics in the Second World War* (New York: Viking-Penguin, 1990). For example, on the day of the Normandy landing, when all of Europe was still in Hitler's hands, Allied air power, the greater part of which was of course American, outnumbered Germany's by a factor of ten.
13. Frank Capra and Anatole Litvak, *Why We Fight*. Produced by the Special Service Division of the War Department, 1942-45. Of particular relevance to our theme is the title of Part Three, "Divide and Conquer." The strategy of dvision is associated, naturally, with Nazism.
14. Among those interned rather than relocated, roughly 43 percent were Japanese American and 56 percent were Americans of German, Italian, or Eastern European descent. Certain German American detainees were kept on Ellis Island through August 1947. [For documents and references, see Major Arthur D. Jacobs's website, www.foitimes.com —Trans.].
15. René Girard, *The Scapegoat*, trans. Yvonne Freccero (1982; Baltimore, MD: Johns Hopkins University Press, 1986). Capital punishment's most extreme expression is lynching. Naturally, we are not justifying lynching, only noting that it avails little to discuss the *juridical* aspect without first attending to the *ritual* one.
16. *Lettere dei condannati a morte della Resistenza europea* ... [Letters from Those in the European Resistance Condemned to Death], <www.romacivica.net/anpiroma/documenti/documenti7.html>, accessed December 28, 2007.
17. Among the most important conditions demanded of a country by the European Union, prior to beginning negotiation towards membership, is that it does not employ capital punishment. In Italy's constitution it is stipulated (in Article 27) that convicts have recourse to re-education; this already excludes from such opportunities those who have been condemned to death.
18. *"My anxiety for the cause of France has become ... concern for her honor ..."* (January 19, 1793).
19. See both Edwin Black, *War against the Weak: Eugenics and America's Campaign to Create a Master Race* (New York: Thunder's Mouth Press, 2003), and Jonathan Glover, *Humanity: A Moral History of the Twentieth Century* (New Haven, CT: Yale University Press, 1999), Chapter 21.

20. Anders Stephanson, *Manifest Destiny: American Expansion and the Empire of Right* (New York: Farrar, Straus & Giroux, 1995).
21. Edwin Black, *War against the Weak.*
22. Erich Neumann, *Depth Psychology and a New Ethic* (1948; Boston, MA: Shambhala, 1990).
23. Walter Benjamin, *Über den Begriff der Geschichte* [On the Idea of History], VII (1942) in *Gesammelte Schriften*, I. 2 (Frankfurt am Main: Suhrkamp, 1989). Referring to Fustel de Coulanges and Flaubert, he remembers that "... il a fallu être triste pour ressusciter Carthage" [one must be melancholy to revive Carthage]. Benjamin believed that this could supersede historical materialism: an example, perhaps, of how such materialism thought it could do without psychology.
24. Peter C. Whybrow, *American Mania: When More Is Not Enough* (New York: W. W. Norton & Company, 2005).
25. The speech in which Benito Mussolini announced to the nation Italy's entry into World War II began with the words: "... La dichiarazione di guerra *è già stata consegnata* agli ambasciatori di Gran Bretagna e di Francia" [the declaration of war already has been delivered to the British and French amabassadors]. Italians were informed of a *fait accompli*, and were notifed of events that had already taken place; they repaid this treatment with the meagerest sort of participation in the conflict.
26. This participation traditionally made American military power capable of sustaining extremely long campaigns; see Tocqueville, *Democracy in America*, vol. II, part 3, ch. XXIV. The abolition of the general military draft and the unexpected evolution of wars such as those in Vietnam and the second Iraq conflict, however, have weakened this tradition.
27. Michael Walzer, *Just and Unjust Wars: A Moral Argument with Historical Illustrations* (New York: Basic Books, 1977).
28. Paul Bairoch, *Victoires et déboires: Histoire économique et sociale du monde du XVI siècle à nos jours, Vol. III* (Paris: Gallimard, 1997), Part 4, Chapter 24.
29. *The Lancet* (online edition for October 12, 2006), which has carried out a cross-sectional cluster sample survey, estimates that around 655,000 residents have died in the Iraq War (in excess of normal), obviously the greater part of them civilians. As of February 2008, the American dead numbered some 3,900. *The New England Journal of Medicine*, using a larger sample, estimates the Iraqi toll from 2003 through to 2006 at 223,000 (upper limit). Comparative estimates of six studies are available in the CRS Report for Congress at www.fas.org/sgp/crs/mideast, and John Tirman reviews the media controversy over these at www.editorandpublisher.com, February 28, 2008. Even when one adopts the lower figures, the ratio of civilian-occupied dead to American military dead registers at an all-time high.
30. Walzer, *Just and Unjust Wars*, Chapters 7 and 8.

31. Besides having written her memoirs of the postwar years, Traudl Junge also gave a film interview to André Heller and Othmar Schmiderer shortly before her death: *Im toten Winkel—Hitlers Sekretärin* [In Death's Corner—Hitler's Secretary], Dor Film Production, 2002.
32. Sophie Scholl was the organizer, along with her brother Hans and other students at the University of Munich, of the resistance cell against Nazism called *The White Rose*. Sophie Scholl was guillotined in February of 1943 at the age of 21.

CHAPTER TWO—TRAUMA AND ABUSE: THE DEVELOPMENT OF A CULTURAL COMPLEX IN THE HISTORY OF LATIN AMERICA

1. S. Cook and W. Borah, *Essays on Population History*, vol. 1 (Berkeley, CA: University of California Press, 1971).
2. Octavio Paz, *El labirinto de la soledad* (1950; Mexico: Fondo de Cultura Economica, 1986).
3. We might call this the "Mexican" interpretation of the events. There is also a "Parisian" one. Todorov emphasizes in his works the novelty and the strength of the scrutiny to which Montezuma and the Mexicans are subjected by Cortes (Tzvetan Todorov, *La conquête de l'Amérique: La question de Vautre* [Paris: Seuil, 1982]; *Récits azteques de la Conquête* [Paris: Seuil, 1983]). In contrast to Columbus, who remains attached to his prejudices, Cortes confronts openly the problem of the *other*: he looks for informants, interpreters, intermediaries. He knows he is facing an absolute novelty and wants to understand it, even if his final goal is one of domination. Serge Gruzinski, in *La colonization de l'imaginaire* (Paris: Gallimard, 1988), suggests a problem of encounter and assimilation: more precisely, the gradual incorporation of the Mexican imagination into the Western and Christian one. Then we have Alicia Dujovne Ortiz (born in Argentina but living in Paris) re-evoking the horrors of the meeting between the two worlds and concluding: "It is not the American continent that became hybrid in 1492: it's the world. … Europe doesn't risk becoming hybrid … it has been so for five centuries, at least in its soul" ("Le mépris, la méprise et le métis," *Magazine Littéraire* 296 [February 1992]: 56-58, trans. V.-P. Stirnimann). The European world speaks of hybridism because it does not have to fear assimilation. The non-European world is afraid of disappearing in the process of giving meaning to this hybridism.
4. I have developed this topic in *Growth and Guilt: Psychology and the Limits of Development* (London: Routledge, 1995).
5. Mircea Eliade, *The Myth of the Eternal Return: Or, Cosmos and History* (Paris, 1949; Princeton, NJ: Princeton University Press, 1971).
6. See Chapter 1, "The Nahuatl conception of time and space," in E. Florescano, *Memoria mexicana* (Mexico: Editorial Joaquin Mortiz, 1988): "The essential

was not the flux of things, but the founding act that had eradicated chaos and created order in the Universe, establishing harmony in the world and conjuring the dangers of its disruption. Which amounts to saying that to maintain order, foundation and duration, all human creations had to repeat the creating act *par excellence*. ... *All* creation is then a repetition of the creation" (p. 29, trans. V.-P. Stirnimann).

7. Todorov, *La conquête de l'Amérique*.
8. The anxiety of inserting the new event into the continuity of all that has already happened—or at least been written about or described—is always and everywhere to be found. Couldn't we see Jungian culture almost as a kind of oral culture transmitted through analysis, never to be entirely comprehended by the written text? And doesn't Jungian culture consist in the rediscovery of this reassurance, this victory of what has been there forever over what is new, a longing for the archetype and its cyclic repetition—even though an individual and individuating one?
9. The relationship between continuity, identity, and a situation of collective conflict has been focused on very well by Renos Papadopoulos, "Individual Identity and Collective Narratives of Conflict," *Harvest* 43, no. 2 (1997).
10. *Ibid.*
11. Giorgio de Santillana, "Fato antico e fato moderno," in *Reflections on Man and Ideas* (1963; Boston, MA: MIT Press, 1968).
12. The Alexandrine Line and the seal *Inter Coetera* from Pope Alexander VI (1493).
13. Las Casas, in his largest work, *Historia de las Indias* (1553-61). See also Todorov, *La conquête de l'Amérique*.
14. Todorov, *Récits azteques de la Conquête.*
15. Diego Muñoz Camargo, *Historia de Tlaxcala*, ed. Luis Reyes Garcia, with Xavier Lira Toledo (Mexico: Gobierno del Estado de Tlaxcala, 1988), Chapter 1. The chapter also includes a detailed list of signs and wonders that supposedly preceded and predicted the Spaniards' arrival.
16. Donald Kalsched, *The Inner World of Trauma* (London: Routledge, 1996).
17. See the classic studies of R. J. Lifton, *Death in Life: Survivors of Hiroshima* (New York: Vintage, 1969), and *Home from War: Vietnam Veterans* (New York: Simon & Schuster, 1973).
18. See Primo Levi, *Se questo e un uomo*, 3rd ed. (Turin: Einaudi, 1958); for Rosenstock, see Odette Abadi, *Terre de détresse* (Paris: L'Harmattan, 1995); and Jean Améry, *Jenseits von Schuld und Sühne. Bewältigungsversuche eines Überwältigten,* 2nd ed. (Stuttgart: Klett, 1977).
19. Paz, *El labirinto de la soledad.*
20. Kalsched, *The Inner World of Trauma.*
21. Paz, p. 4.
22. Primo Levi, "Le nostre notti," in *Se questo e un uomo*; see also the epigraph of *La tregua*, published in the same volume.

23. Elie Wiesel, *La nuit* (Paris: Éditions de Minuit, 1958).
24. *Codice Florentino*. Ediciòn del Gobierno de la Repùblica [Mexicana], 3 vols. (Mexico City, 1980). *The Florentine Codex* [1540-1585, ed. Bernardino de Sahagun: Nahautl and Spanish facing texts], Book XI, trans. J. O. Arthur and Charles E. D. Anderson, 12 vols., University of Utah Press (1952-1975), Book 11, 1963.
25. *Ibid.*, XX.
26. *Ibid.*, VI.

CHAPTER THREE—THE DUEL AND HONOR

1. Konrad Lorenz, *On Aggression* (1966) 2nd ed. (London: Routledge, 2002). [Originally published as *Das sogennante Böse: Zur Naturgeschichte der Aggression* (1963)].
2. The Polish-born historian of international law Theodor Meron has made an extensive study of the pre-existing basis for modern laws of war in the codes of honor in Shakespeare's plays. These codes, he points out, are mostly survivals of classical rules of combat filtered through Christian culture. See *Henry's Wars and Shakespeare's Laws: Perspectives on the Law of War in the Later Middle Ages* (New York: Oxford University Press, 1994), and *Bloody Constraint: War and Chivalry in Shakespeare* (New York: Oxford University Press, 1998).
3. Lucien Fèbvre, "Honneur et Patrie" (1945-1946), Lecture 6 (Paris: Perrin, 1996).
4. Arnold Hauser, *The Social History of Art* (1951) 3rd ed. (London: Routledge, 1999), Vol. 1.4.8.
5. Jean Flori, *Chevaliers et chevalerie au Moyen Âge* (Paris: Hachette, 1998), Part 2.2. Both the bow and crossbow were reserved for common foot soldiers, but certain papal documents, together with the Lateran Council of 1139, banned their use by all Christians!
6. See, for example, Chapter 7 of Johan Huizinga's classic, *The Waning of the Middle Ages: A Study of the Forms of Life, Thought, and Art in France and the Netherlands in the XIVth and XVth Centuries* (1919)(New York: St. Martin's Press, 1984).
7. *Ibid.*, Chapters 6 and 7.
8. Meron, *Henry's Wars*, Chapter 7, and Huizinga, *Waning of the Middle Ages*, Chapter 7.
9. Torquato Tasso, *Gerusalemme liberata* (1581), Canto 12:53.
10. Sir Walter Scott, *Ivanhoe* (1819), Vol. 1, Chapter 8.
11. Fèbvre, "Honneur et Patrie," Lecture 3.
12. Memorandum to the heads of state by Pope Benedict XV, August 1, 1917 (available at the Vatican website, www.totustuus.org).
13. These episodes are more easily recovered from original documents, such as soldiers' mail, than from the histories of the time, which are dominated by

nationalism and its offshoot, fascism. See, for instance, L. Spitzer's *Lettere di prigioneri di guerra italiani* (1915-1918) (Turin: Boringhieri, 1976).

14. Alexis de Tocqueville, *Democracy in America* (1835),Vol. 2, Part 3, Chapter 18, "Honor in the United States and in Democratic Societies" [*De l'honneur aux États-Unis et dans les sociétés démocratiques*], trans. Gerald Bevan (New York: Penguin Classics, 2003).
15. See James Bowman, *Honor: A History* (New York: Encounter Books, 2006).

CHAPTER FOUR—NIGHTMARES

1. Burkert reminds us that, whatever the epoch, human cooperation comes into being everywhere much more through the common channeling of aggressions than of benevolent attitudes, which bring people together in a limited fashion and only for brief intervals. The violence of attacking and killing together seems to extend and reinforce the initial cooperation of the chase (Walter Burkert, *Homo Necans: The Anthropology of Ancient Greek Sacrificial Ritual and Myth*, trans. Peter Bing (Berlin: de Gruyter, 1972; Berkeley, CA: University of California, 1983), Chapter 1, Secs. 3-6. René Girard studies the unifying function of identifying and ritually killing the scapegoat: *The Scapegoat* (Paris: Grasset & Fasquelle, 1982; Baltimore, MD: Johns Hopkins University Press, 1989), and the centrality of murder in foundation myths (see: *I See Satan Fall like Lightning* [Paris: Grasset & Fasquelle, 1999; New York: Orbis, 2001], Chapter 7, "The Founding Murder"). According to Wolfgang Giegerich, the killing, first of animals always larger than men, and then of other human beings, is a foundational stage in building the conscious center of the psychic activity that psychoanalysis calls the ego (*Tötungen: Gewalt aus der Seele: Versuch über Ursprung und Geschichte des Bewüsstseins* [Frankfurt: Peter Lang, 1994]).
2. C. G. Jung, *The Collected Works of C. G. Jung*, trans. R. F. C. Hull, ed. H. Read, M. Fordham, G. Adler, Wm. McGuire, 20 vols. (Princeton, NJ: Princeton University Press, 1953-1979), Vol. 5, § 370-373.
3. See Karl Jaspers, *Allgemeine Psychopathologie* (1923); Eugen Bleuler, *Lehrbuch der Psychiatrie* (1991); Henri Ey, *Manuel de psychiatrie* (Paris: Masson, 1960, 1989); *The Harvard Guide to Modern Psychiatry*, ed. Armand M. Nicholi, Jr. (Cambridge, MA: Harvard University Press, 1980); Silvano Arieti, ed., *American Handbook of Psychiatry* (1959, 1966).
4. *Diagnostic and Statistical Manual of Mental Disorders* (Washington, D.C.: American Psychiatric Association, 1994).
5. Other summarized data have been furnished by J. F. Pagel, "Nightmares and Disorders of Dreaming," *American Family Physician* 61 (2000): 2037-2042.
6. Personal communication from Rita Skolek-Winnisch, of the Faculty of Veterinary Medicine at the University of Vienna.
7. Herodotus, *Histories* 7.56.

8. We often forget that the psychoanalyst, who seems to love the dream, is in a kind of negation, another escape. The dream, and its limit-phenomenon, the nightmare, mean something of the same thing to us. But this meaning stays internal to oneiric logic and reality, which remains only feebly grounded when we discuss it on waking. Jacques Derrida has said (in his lecture on accepting the Adorno Prize at Frankfurt, November 22, 2001, "La Langue de l'étranger," repr. *Fichus: Discours de Francfort* [Paris, Galilée, 2002]): "Could a dreamer … talk about his dream without waking?" The traditional answer from philosophy and Western science is potentially a "No," while a more comprehensive answer—more psychoanalytic, we might add—would have to include a "Sometimes," a "Perhaps," and of course a frank "Yes."
9. Of interest to our theme is the welcome given to this idea by the general public. The theory that humans are a homicidal derivative of apes was put forth in the mid-20th century as a specialized study by the Australian paleontologist Raymond Dart, but reached the general public—still obsessed with the human evil revealed in World War II—in the 1961 best-seller by Robert Ardrey, *African Genesis*, and in the 1968 film by Stanley Kubrick, *2001: A Space Odyssey.*
10. The most famous treatment of this theme is the one set forth by Konrad Lorenz in *Das sogennante Böse: Zur Naturgeschichte der Aggression* (1963) (*On Aggression* [New York: Harcourt Brace, 1966; 2nd ed., London: Routledge, 2002]).
11. Iräneus Eibl-Eibesfeldt, *Die Biologie des menschlichen Verhatlens* (Munich: Piper, 1984), Parts 1 and 4. Eibl-Eibesfeldt credits Erik Erikson with first having articulated this concept.
12. "There is a notorious biological racism among the social animals." Primo Levi, "Why no comeback for the holocausts of yesteryear?" in *La Stampa*, 10 May 1979.
13. Iräneus Eibl-Eibesfeldt, *Etologia della guerra* (1979) (Turin: Boringhieri, 1990).
14. Anthony Pagden, *The Fall of Natural Man: The American Indian and the Origins of Comparative Ethnology,* Cambridge Iberian and Latin American Studies (Cambridge, UK: Cambridge University Press, 1982). Cf. also his *European Encounters with the New World; From Renaissance to Romanticism* (New Haven: Yale University Press, 1994).
15. Michelangelo Jacobucci, *I nemici del dialogo: Ragione e perversioni dell' intolleranza* (Rome: Armando, 2005).
16. *Ibid.*, Preface by Ecco.
17. Till Bastian, *Das Jahrhundert des Todes* (Göttingen: Vandenhoeck & Ruprecht, 2000). The Kaiser's speech is quoted on p. 74. Given at Bremerhaven in July of 1900, it had caused a stir in Europe already before World War I. See *The Kaiser's Speeches, Forming a Character Portrait of Emperor William II,* trans. Wolf von Schierbrand (New York & London: Harper & Brothers, 1903), pp. 256-260.
18. *Ibid.*, p. 187.

19. This rapid development threw into relief how the camps, and the act of amassing huge numbers of people, are inventions of the 20th century. Marco Deriu—drawing upon Zygmunt Baumann and Giorgio Agamben, among others—develops one of the fullest testimonies we have in his *Dizionario critico delle nuove guerre* [Critical Dictionary of Modern Wars] (Bologna: EMI, 2005). This important analytical history should be rounded out with a psychological one. The establishment of the camps presupposes a kind of insurmountable difference, accompanied by contempt, mistrust, and paranoia. Such is not the case in the first camps established among the most brutal colonial enterprises at the end of the 19th century (Cuba and the Philippines). In the 20th century, however, the number and types of such camps exploded in Europe. A continuity began that makes it difficult to distinguish the slaughters brought about in concentration camps from those that happened during "transit" to concentration, whether in camps for prisoners of war or political prisoners, or camps for ethnic groups, re-education, or, finally, extermination. The psychological feeling about otherness or difference, historically a "given" with colonialism, came to be artificially constructed in Europe by psychological warfare and by campaigns of nationalistic and class hatred. The conviction of irremediable difference and superiority—which is the foundational presupposition for choosing to build the camps, and becomes the shared patrimony of the captors—is also the principal obstacle in the way of functioning not only humanly but even rationally. And it is also the factor that drives all other types of camps towards a creeping transformation into death camps. If we are wholly convinced that the other person is subhuman, why waste energy, oversight, food rations, and barbed wire? If homicide is the killing of humans, the killing of subhumans cannot be homicide, but something else.
20. Niall Ferguson, *The Pity of War* (1998) (New York: Basic Books, 1999), Chapter 13.
21. Angelo Del Boca, *Italiani brava gente?* (Vicenza: Neri Pozza, 2005), Chapter 6.
22. Herb Kutchins and Stuart A. Kirk, *Making Us Crazy: DSM—The Psychiatric Bible and the Creation of Mental Disorders* (New York: Free Press, 1999), Chapter 4. Without going into detail, it is worth taking the trouble to note that the use of psychiatry as an adjunct to military force has a tradition with many ramifications in the United States. The poet Ezra Pound, who broadcast propaganda against his country during World War II, was classified as a psychiatric case in lieu of standing trial for treason, and was confined to a hospital for the insane.
23. I refer not only to Roman mythology, which speaks literally of Furies, but also to situations described, for example, by Homer. The duel between Hector and Achilles (*Iliad* 22)—in which the Greek refuses not only to concede mercy, but also to respect his enemy's corpse, which he abandons to the wolves—can stand for all of them.

24. To imagine the contribution that a more courageous psychiatry might make, it is enough to note that, even today, the most influential critique of colonialism remains that of a psychiatrist: Frantz Fanon's *The Wretched of the Earth* (Paris: Maspero, 1961, with a preface by Sartre; New York: Grove Press, 1963, 2005). Fanon died at only 36; one can scarcely imagine the level his contribution to the pathology of history might have reached if he had not disappeared at an age at which hardly any psychiatrist or psychoanalyst has managed to publish something significant (Freud, for example, published his first real work, *The Interpretation of Dreams*, at 43).
25. Kutchins and Kirk, *Making Us Crazy*.
26. This points to the objective of killing civilians by terrorizing them and choking the back roads of the enemy's country with disordered flight. See Massimo L. Salvadori, ed., *Encyclopedia of History* (Bologna: Zanichelli, 2000), and M. Deriu, *Dizionario critico delle nuove guerre*. The best-known example is the indiscriminate aerial bombardment of metropolitan centers during World War II, aimed at breaking the resistance of the civilian population, and employed by all parties to the conflict but carried out in the great majority of instances by the British and Americans.
27. Carole Beebe Tarantelli, "Life within Death: Towards a Metapsychology of Catastrophic Psychic Trauma," *International Journal of Psychoanalysis* 84 (2003): 915-923. Levi's nightmares are described in the chapter "Our Nights," in *If This Is a Man* (Turin: Einaudi, 1958; New York: Everyman's Library, 2000).

CHAPTER FIVE—REDUCTIVISM: AGAINST ISMENE

1. For a transcript of this speech by Lagos Escobar, see www.usal.es/gabinete/protocolo. Lagos Escobar was president of Chile from 2000 to 2005, and was awarded the *laurea honoris causa* at the University of Salamanca October 10, 2005. He took up an appointment as professor-at-large at Brown University and the Watson Institute in 2007.
2. See Pastore Ferruccio, *Dobbiamo Temere le Migrazioni?* [Should We Be Afraid of Migration?] (Bari, Italy: Laterza, 2004).
3. Machiavelli, *Discourses on the First Ten Books of Livy* (1531), 3.1.
4. See Luigi Zoja, *Cultivating the Soul* (London: Free Association Books, 2005), especially Part Two, Chapter Eight ("Individuation and Paideia"), and all of Part Four ("Tragic Thought").
5. Luigi Zoja, *Ethics & Analysis: Philosophical Perspectives and Their Application in Therapy* (College Station, TX: Texas A&M University Press, 2007).
6. See Jacob Burckhardt, *Die Kultur der Renaissance in Italien* [The Civilization of the Renaissance in Italy] (1860).
7. See Antonietta Haddad, *Freud en Italie: Psychanalyse du voyage* (Paris: Albin Michel, 1995). See also Graziella Magherini, *La Sindrome de Stendhal* (Florence: Ponte alle Grazie, 1989).

8. Augustine, *Confessions* 6.3.
9. Gregg Easterbrook, *The Progress Paradox* (New York: Random House, 2003).
10. Dante, *De Monarchia*, Book I.
11. In *The United States Democratic Review* 6, no. 23 (November 1839): 426-430.
12. Horace, *Odes* 1.11.8; Lorenzo de Medici, *The Triumph of Bacchus and Ariadne*, a carnival song-poem written in about 1475.
13. See H. van Praag, *Can We Live with Business?* (Utrecht: University College Utrecht, 2005).
14. See Eugène Minkowski, *Le temps vécu* (1933).
15. Philippe Ariès, *Western Attitudes toward Death: From the Middle Ages to the Present* (Baltimore, MD: Johns Hopkins University Press, 1975).
16. Geoffrey Gorer, "The Pornography of Death" (1955), reprinted in Geoffrey Gorer, *Death, Grief, and Mourning* (Garden City, NY: Doubleday, 1965).
17. See C. G. Jung, "On Psychological Understanding" (1914), CW 3, § 391, and "On Psychic Energy" (1928), CW 8, § 94-95 in *The Collected Works of C. G. Jung*, trans. R. F. C. Hull, ed. H. Read, M. Fordham, G. Adler, Wm. McGuire, 20 vols. (Princeton, NJ: Princeton University Press, 1953-1979).
18. Jung, *CW* 13, § 54.

CHAPTER SIX—THE CLASH OF CIVILIZATIONS? A STRUGGLE BETWEEN IDENTITY AND FUNCTIONALISM

1. Elias Canetti, *Die gespaltene Zukunft: Aufsätze und Gespräche* [The Dissociated Future: Essays and Speeches] (Munich: Hanser, 1972), p. 1.
2. James Hillman's definition, employed at the same conference, *"E' Scontro di Civiltà?"* as noted above.
3. From 1910 to 2000, that is, in only ninety years, the White population of New York City has declined from 98 percent to only 35 percent (see the tables published in the *New York Times*, March 16, 2001, Section B, pp. 6-7). In the second decade of the 21st century it should decline to approximately one quarter of the whole. This genuine revolution is accompanied by social problems, not by cultural or ethnic clashes.
4. René Girard, *The Scapegoat* [*Le bouc émissaire* (1982)] (Baltimore, MD: Johns Hopkins University Press, 1989).
5. In psychotherapeutic relationships, for example, where the question is whether or not the transference survives sessions that are carried out in teleconferencing or on a chat-line.
6. See a sociological analysis of this problem in Zygmunt Baumann, *Society under Siege* (Cambridge, UK: Polity Press, 2002). I have touched on this theme in *La morte del prossimo* (currently in progress).

7. James Hillman, "On Culture and Chronic Disorder," the inaugural lecture at the Dallas Institute of Humanities and Culture, 1981, published in *The Institute Newsletter* 1, no. 2 (February-March 1982).
8. Aristotle, *Politics* 7.1326a-b.
9. Hermann Diels, *Die Fragmente der Vorsokratiker* [Pre-Socratic Fragments], ed. Walther Kranz (Berlin: Weidmann, 1974), fragment 60 (my translation).
10. For example, the extremely interesting but controversial Gavin Menzies, in *1421: The Year China Discovered America* (2002) (New York: HarperCollins Publishers, 2004), Chapter 1.
11. Zhang Qizhi, ed., *Traditional Chinese Culture* (Beijing: Foreign Languages Press, 2004), Chapter 11.
12. For the PNAC document, see www.newamericancentury.org. As for the chronology between Fukuyama and Huntington, whereas Fukuyama's text was written after the fall of the Berlin Wall, in 1992, Huntington published under this title for the first time in 1993, in the journal *Foreign Affairs*, in response to Fukuyama (and followed this up with a book in 1996). Therefore, we are dealing with an analysis that was originally rather specialized, but was subsequently rolled out on new wheels in response to the attacks on the Twin Towers and the Pentagon.
13. See Chapter Two, above. "Trauma and Abuse."
14. Herodotus, *The Histories*, trans. Aubrey de Sélincourt (New York: Penguin Classics, 1972), p. 42.
15. For such a complex problem it is possible to use only simple examples. In one of the most memorable speeches—memorable for its contribution to fueling global anti-American sentiment—George W. Bush spoke of a *crusade* against the Islamic [terrorist] threat. Naturally, he immediately tried to rectify the situation so as not to offer the impression that he wished to revive the conflict between Islam and the West that began in the preceding millennium. The incident was closed as if it were an unwitting mistake, helped along by the president's proverbial ignorance. But Freud has shown that the personal unconscious does not make casual mistakes. In their turn, too, the collective unconscious and its narratives pre-exist any individual expressions of them.
16. It is interesting to reconstruct how psychologists came to find themselves in the torture chamber. For some time the CIA had run the approved programs of SERE (Survival, Evasion, Resistance, and Escape), in which military personnel were taught how, if captured by an enemy, to resist treatment that violated the Geneva Conventions pertaining to combatants. But, in terms of technique, why not turn this approach upside down and use the experience to deal with prisoners who, by happy coincidence, are not protected by the Geneva Conventions? The magical notion is to do a bit of reverse engineering, inverting technology, just as with a mechanism that one can run in one direction or the other. Naturally, if interrogation is morally neutral, then it may also be

put out on contract. And so it happened that reductive subcontracting assigned these interrogations to private agencies (security firms) run by psychologists.

17. See Chapter One, above: "Violent Hearts."

CHAPTER SEVEN—ALMACHIUS AND THE DEMON

1. *Archeo* XIII.11 (1997), "Lo spettacolo comincia. Il teatro nel mondo Greco e romano," p. 76.
2. Genesis 32:23-33.
3. Horace, Epistles 2.1 l.156: "Graecia capta ferum victorem coepit et artes intulit agresti Latio."
4. Thucydides, *The Peloponnesian War*, II.38, trans. Benjamin Jowett, in *The Greek Historians*, Vol.1, ed. Frederick Godolphin (New York: Random House, 1942), p. 649.
5. "Bread and circuses," [*panem et circenses*], Juvenal, *Satires* 10, l.81.
6. Terence, *Hecyra*, Prologue II, ll. 33-42.
7. Mary Beard and Keith Hopkins, *The Colosseum* (Cambridge, MA: Harvard University Press 2005). Martial's *De spectaculis* lists many spectacles held in the Flavian Amphitheater, but follows a sequence that is more poetic than chronological.
8. According to Cassius Dio, the inauguration of the amphitheater occasioned the deaths of 9,000 animals. However, his assertions are often exaggerated: in connection with the Colosseum, he reports that it was flooded in order to stage a naval battle, a claim to which few today lend credence.
9. Max Weber, "Politics as a Vocation" ["Politik als Beruf" (lecture, 1919)], in *From Max Weber: Essays in Sociology*, trans. and ed. H. H. Gerth and C. Wright Mills (New York: Oxford University Press, 1958), pp. 77-128.
10. This practice introduced a few variants, always in order to meet practical exigencies. It is difficult to have an eagle assault a man, as required by the myth. And so the criminal Laureolus, who stood in for Prometheus, was offered up to a bear, which ate him alive, piece by piece: *De spectaculis* vii.
11. *De spectaculis* v. Pasiphae, the wife of King Minos of Crete, according to the myth, fell in love with a bull and commissioned Daedalus to construct a cow mannequin for her, into which she could climb in order to copulate with the bull. From this monstrous union was born the Minotaur, a mythical monster half bull and half man.
12. The few testimonies that we have lead us to think that by the end of a typical day at the games the dead gladiators amounted not to half their number, as statistics would have it with duels to the death, but between 1/5 and 1/6. This has its own logic, because even professional gladiators were worth a fortune, and the master of the games, as the impresario who invested in the spectacle, was not willing to be seen killing them off too quickly.

13. Carlin Barton, *The Sorrow of the Ancient Romans*, Chapter One. Princeton, NJ: Princeton University Press , 1996.
14. In Thucydides's words (*The Peloponnesian War*, II.46), spoken by Pericles at the end of his funeral eulogy after the first year of fighting, the life of Athens promoted excellence or αρετη, *arête*—"virtues."
15. Of the two names by which this monk is known, Telemachus and Almachius, I prefer the second, because the first might be confused with that of Odysseus's son. In reality, both names may be successive adjuncts or honorifics. *Almachios* may be associated with the Latin *almus* (nurse or benefactress, typically in the title *Alma Mater* given to Mary), in turn derived from the verb *alo*, to feed), along with a place name (perhaps the island of Chios).
16. The principal source of the information about Almachius was compiled in the writings of Theodoret, born in Antioch and later the bishop of Cyrus: Τεοδωρητου, επισκοπου Κυρου, *Απαντα, Patrologiae Graecae*, vol. 82, p. 1068, col. 26.
17. Fragmentum Laureshamensis ed Epternacensis.
18. "... και του τοισ αιμασιν εκεινοισ επιτερπομενου δαιμονοσ εισδεξαμενοι (Theodoret, *Patrolgiae Graecae*, vol. 82, p. 1067, col. 26B; emphasis mine). The premodern narrative confuses our modern psychological, theological, and ethical perspectives. The event is monstrous, but who is responsible? The populace, or the demon who stirs them up, or the frenzy—a personficiation within a personficiation, "frenzy" stemming from *phrena* or mind—that possessed the demon?
19. *Macbeth*, V. v. 27-28.
20. Maria Sahuillo, "Sin matar, falta algo en las corridas," *El Pais*, August 8, 2007, p. 2. (It is an article I kept last year, then lost, then found again.) See also Dan Bilefsky, "The Portuguese matador who crossed the red line," *International Herald Tribune*, August 12, 2007, pp. 1, 4.
21. After the judgment against Pedrito, from motives of "popular tradition and culture" (Sahuillo), the Portuguese authorities began to allow the killing of bulls in the arena at Barrancos. Today numberless Internet sites replay Pedrito's feat, and on YouTube one may admire the elegance with which he stands up to the bull. But it is difficult to imagine that similar film clips would achieve comparable distribution if they failed to include the animal's death.
22. Matthew 27:16-17.
23. Luke 23:19.
24. "Rabbi," John 1:38.
25. Theodoret of Cyrus.
26. Krummes Holz, "Immanuel Kant, Idee zu einer allgemeinen Geschichte in weltbürglicher Absicht" (1784), in *Akademische Ausgabe*, vol. 8, p. 23.

AFTERWORD—ZOJA AMONG OTHERS: BETWEEN THE EGO AND A HARD PLACE

1. Walter Burkert, *Homo Necans: The Anthropology of Ancient Greek Sacrificial Ritual and Myth*, trans. Peter Bing (Berkeley, CA: University of California Press, 1983), p. 22.
2. To cite only the crudely material factor behind this common mayhem: at the time of writing, an estimated 250 million guns circulate in the USA, whose adult population is around 293 million. Almost democratic!
3. In Chapter 5 here, "Reductivism: Against Ismene," Zoja cites the high incidence of suicide among veterans of Argentina's Falkland Islands War against Thatcher's Britain. In reversed ratios, the Malvine Campaign and the Iraq Invasion share one factor, in their asymmetrical terms of engagement. Suicide rates among U.S. combat troops still on duty in the occupation have mounted steeply (as of early 2008), as they had already been high among returning veterans (currently 120 per week). As of now, the Bush regime is pressing to cut mental health benefits for veterans, by administrative determinations not subject to legal review (B. Egelko, "Veterans Denied," *San Francisco Chronicle*, February 5, 2008).
4. Let me anticipate certain other of Zoja's themes while ballasting my opening recollection. In Chapter 4, "Nightmares," Zoja reviews the rise and subsequent history of "military psychiatry," dissecting the complex shame that its practices have brought on Western countries beginning even before World War I. The strongly felt measures addressed by the old Greeks to the contaminating power of killing, both in and out of battle (see "The Shedding of Blood," Ch. 4 of Robert Parker, *Miasma: Pollution and Purification in Greek Religion* [Oxford, UK: Oxford University Press, 1983]), leaves Aeschylus a better medic than our own. That is, an ancient society in many ways remote from ours (half Viking, half Japanese, as Guy Davenport said), got closer to facts, from which we maintain a certain distance, by insisting on binding root and branch together.

   Page du Bois's *Torture and Truth* (London: Routledge, 1991) reminds us that even the Socratic *elenchus* or investigation mimics the torture of slaves in pursuit of reliable testimony. Our unease about that to one side, Greeks of the city-state resolved to begin to master human violence. The *Oresteia* ends with the establishment of a court system that could address demonic family vendettas by reassigning the Furies to somewhat buffered roles. The Choes festival described by Burkert betokens a communal awareness of what anthropology now underlines, namely, the foundational murderousness that cements the civic compact itself. By staging things when the new wine comes in, that Athenian ritual ties Dionysian descent into the very knot of foundational killing. No such apotropaic and re-balancing practice, unless it be Nijinsky's solitary dance of "The War" in 1919 as he descended into madness, has played a part in our civilization.

5. Two of Zoja's moral themes in these essays stay closely linked: responsibility, and then the time required for guilt and meaning to lend weight to responsibility. The immunity patch in my figure of speech addresses one American trait in particular, the will not to perceive costs and consequences over long periods of time. Let me cite two instances, one broad and long and the other narrower and recent.

   First: Through indices used by social scientists both here and abroad, the USA is the most intensely nationalistic and corporatist of the developed nations, while also being the most convinced of its exceptional, benevolent mission. These attitudes have largely consigned any consequent awareness of the country's past century of overt and covert policies of violent intervention—throughout Central and Latin America, and elsewhere from the Philippines, Jakarta, Mossadegh's Iran, to tiny Diego Garcia—to the unconscious.

   Second: After the 2003 aggression against Iraq, the USA for five years has avoided any reckoning with the most reliable estimates of Iraqi dead and exiled (the Lancet-Johns Hopkins Study of 2005, the U.K. ORB Report of 2007, and the relatively muted Iraq Ministry of Heath Report of 2007). Between 2005 and 2007, statistics point reliably to somewhere between 600,000 and over 1,000,000 civilian casualties from the occupation, and at least 2,000,000 exiled.

   This collective will to blot out costs and consequences over time is keenly shadowed by the will to go on oppressing former enemies, notably Native Americans and the Vietnamese (see Amy den Ouden, *Beyond Conquest: Native Peoples and the Struggle for History in New England* [Lincoln, NE: University of Nebraska Press, 2005], and Edwin Martini, *Invisible Enemies: The American War on Vietnam, 1975-2000* [Amherst, MA: University of Massachusetts Press, 2000]).
6. Zoja's reflections on guilt, honor, and the traumatic burden of modern wars occur in his first, third, and fourth chapters here. Compare these to Anthony Stevens in his *The Roots of War and Terror* (New York: Continuum, 2004), p. 171. What Stevens says of the Vietnam mission applies also to Iraq and the battalion that chorused "Satan!" at Fallujah before destroying it in 2005: "Their leaders failed to call out collective superego projections of adequate strength to free the men from the guilt of killing." The fact of miasma (see Parker, *Miasma*) remains tolerable only when archetypal animosity wears boots issued by reliably accountable intent.
7. See Chapter 4, "James Hillman's Revolution," in Luigi Zoja, *Cultivating the Soul*, trans. John Peck, Mark Kyburz, Henry Martin, Anthony Molino, Christine Ware (London: Free Association Books, 2005) [*Coltivare l'anima* (Bergamo: Moretti & Vitali, 1999)].
8. *Jungian Reflections on September 11: A Global Nightmare*, ed. Luigi Zoja and Donald Williams (Einsiedeln, Switzerland: Daimon Verlag, 2002); *L'incubo*

globale: Prospettive Junghiane a proposito dell' 11 Settembre, ed. Luigi Zoja, trans. Luciano Perez (Bergamo: Moretti & Vitali, 2002). Roberto Buffagni's essay is "Con gli occhi di un occidentale," pp. 204-214.

9. Various exemplars: French demographer Emmanuel Todd, *After the Empire: The Breakdown of the American Order*, trans. Jon Delogu (New York: Columbia University Press, 2003); Australian journalist John Pilger, *The New Rulers of the World* (London: Verso, 2003); American writer Carol Brightman, *Total Insecurity: The Myth of American Omnipotence* (London: Verso, 2004); French architect and planner Paul Virilio, *The Paul Virilio Reader*, ed. Steve Redhead (New York: Columbia University Press, 2005); English dramatist Harold Pinter, *Nobel Lecture: Art, Truth and Politics*, 2005.
10. Luigi Zoja, "September 11: Transatlantic Reflections," in Zoja and Williams, *Jungian Reflections*, p. 46.
11. Luigi Zoja, *Growth and Guilt: Psychology and the Limits of Development*, trans. Henry Martin (London: Routledge, 1995), p. 173. (Originally published as *Crescita e colpa*, Milan, 1993.)
12. *Ibid.*
13. Susan Falludi, *The Terror Dream: Fear and Fantasy in Post-9/11 America* (New York: Holt, 2007).
14. Charlotte Beradt, *The Third Reich of Dreams*, trans. Adriane Gottwald, afterword by Bruno Bettelheim (Chicago, IL: Quadrangle Books, 1968) [Nymphenburg, 1966].
15. Doug Grow, "Q&A with whistle-blower Daniel Ellsberg," *Minneapolis Star Tribune*, February 21, 2008. This statement has been Ellsberg's constant refrain, his Greek-chorus summary of the chief learning that informs his *Secrets: A Memoir of Vietnam and the Pentagon Papers* (New York: Viking, 2002). See "A Coup Has Occurred," a speech at the American University, D.C. Symposium of September 20, 2007 (www.counterpunch.com, September 27, 2007, or www.consortiumnews.com, September 26, 2007). Such false honor creates powerful bonds, Ellsberg discovered: after he had violated that relationship, most of his Rand Corporation coworkers did not contact him for twenty-five years.
16. Nicola Chiaromonte, *The Worm of Consciousness and Other Essays*, ed. Miriam Chiaromonte (New York: Harcourt Brace Jovanovich, 1976), and *The Paradox of History: Stendhal, Tolstoy, Pasternak, and Others* (Philadelphia, PA: University of Pennsylvania Press, 1985). Iris Origo, *A Need to Testify: Four Portraits: Portraits of Lauro de Bosis, Ruth Draper, Gaetano Salvemini, Ignazio Silone* (London: John Murray, 1984). Elémire Zolla, *The Eclipse of the Intellectual*, trans. Raymond Rosenthal (New York: Funk & Wagnalls, 1968).
17. The model question attributed to Salvemini by his students ran, "That is what you want to say, isn't it?" See Origo, *A Need to Testify*, pp. 130-131.
18. Luigi Zoja, *The Father: Historical, Psychological, and Cultural Perspectives*, trans. Henry Martin (London: Brunner-Routledge, 2001). (Originally published

as *Il gesto di ettore; Preistoria, storia, attualitá e scomparsa del padre* [Turin: Boringhiere, 2000]).

19. George L. Mosse, *The Crisis of German Ideology: Intellectual Origins of the Third Reich* (New York: Grosset & Dunlap, 1964).
20. Zoja, *The Father*, pp. 19-20.
21. Joseph Henderson, "The Foot-Race for a Prize," in *The Cultural Complex: Contemporary Jungian Perspectives on Psyche and Society*, ed. Thomas Singer and Samuel Kimbles (London: Brunner-Routledge, 2004), pp. 62-63. On the cultural unconscious, see Henderson's earlier *Cultural Attitudes in Psychological Perspective* (Toronto: Inner City, 1993). Zoja's first book was *Drugs, Addiction, and Initiation: The Modern Search for Ritual* (Boston, MA: Sigo, 1989; 2nd ed., Einsiedeln, Switzerland: Daimon Verlag, 2000).

    Useful for a unified view of the depth-psychological background for Zoja's political psychology is Thomas Kirsch, "Cultural Complexes in the History of Jung, Freud, and their Followers," in Singer and Kimbles, *The Cultural Complex*, pp. 185-196.
22. Anthony Stevens, *Archetype Revisited: An Updated Natural History of the Self* (London: Brunner-Routledge, 2002), p. 185.
23. Zoja, *The Father*, pp. 185ff.
24. Zoja, "Individuation and Paideia," in *Cultivating the Soul*.
25. This large theme in commentaries on Plato perhaps best begins with Friedrich Solmsen's inventories of what *psukhē* meant to Homer and the tragedians. See "Plato and the Concept of the Soul (*Psyche*)," *Journal of the History of Ideas* 44/3 (1983): 355-367, and "Phren, Kardia, Psukhe in Greek Tragedy," in *Greek Poetry and Philosophy; Studies in Honour of Leonard Woodbury*, ed. Douglas Gerber (Chico, CA: Scholars Press, 1984).
26. Claudia Barrachi, *Of Myth, Life, and War in Plato's Republic* (Bloomington, IN: Indiana University Press, 2002), p. 165.
27. Paul Crook, *Darwinism, War and History: The Debate over the Biology of War from the 'Origin of Species' to the First World War* (Cambridge, UK: Cambridge University Press, 1994), p. 195.
28. Wolfgang Giegerich, "Killings: Psychology's Platonism and the Missing Link to Reality," *Spring* 54 (June 1993), and "The Invention of Explosive Power and the Blueprint of the Bomb: A Chapter in the Imaginal Pre-History of Our Nuclear Predicament" (1988), in *Technology and the Soul: Collected English Papers*, vol. 2 (New Orleans, LA: Spring Journal Books, 2007), pp. 101-116.
29. See the summary of Saayman's work in his letter to Zoja after his election as honorary member of the IAAP, in *IAAP Newsletter* 22 (2002). There he comments on Jung's pioneer anticipation of ethology and psychobiology, particularly in the seminar on kundalini yoga and its animal symbolism in the early 1930s.
30. Marie-Louise von Franz, "The Transformed Berserk: Unification of Psychic Opposites," in *Human Survival and Consciousness Evolution*, ed. Stanislav

Grof and Marjorie Valier (Albany, NY: SUNY Press, 1988), pp. 28, 34-35. (Collected in von Franz, *Archetypal Dimensions of the Psyche* [Boston, MA: Shambhala, 1997/1999].)

31. Donald Kalsched, "The Roots of War: A Jungian Perspective," *Quadrant* 23/2 (1990): 103-106.
32. The first version (unavailable to me), *The Roots of War: A Jungian Perspective*, is from Paragon House, USA, 1989. *The Roots of War and Terror* (2004), cited above, appears to revise this. Kalsched reviews the 1989 version. This note refers to the 2004 version, p. 238.
33. John Dourley, "Archetypal Hatred as Social Bond: Strategies for Its Dissolution," in *Terror, Violence and the Impulse to Destroy: Perspectives from Analytical Psychology (Papers from the 2002 North American Conference of Jungian Analysts and Candidates)*, ed. John Beebe (Einsiedeln, Switzerland: Daimon Verlag, 2003), pp. 156, 155.
34. See p. 100 below. Zoja's note refers to a 1982 lecture of Hillman's, which may also be found as "Cultural Disorder," in *A Blue Fire: The Essential James Hillman* (London: Routledge & Kegan Paul, 1990), pp. 163-165.
35. Hillman's distinction between culture and civilization seems to stem from Nietzsche's first major work, *On the Advantage and Disadvantage of History for Life* (1874), section 10: "[C]ulture can only grow and blossom out of life" rather than being "tacked on like a paper flower" (trans. Peter Preuss [Indianapolis, IN: Hackett, 1980], p. 59). The distinction rises from *Lebensphilosophie*, to run on a parallel line in Jung and Hillman, and perhaps to claim a descendant in Zoja's revival of the unifying Greek sense of good/beautiful or *kalokagathía*. Zoja's simile between Greek *paideia* and the best fruits of depth analysis implies in milder form Nietzsche's view of modern education, whose "result, viewed in a mean empirical way, is the historical-aesthetic cultural philistine [*Bildungsphilister*]" (*ibid.*). Analysis in that light is both culture and a critique of education in the modern mass democracies, not simply a wholesome dietary supplement.
36. Stevens, *Archetype Revisited*, p. 55.
37. See Hillman's "Culture and the Animal Soul," in *American Soul—Spring* 62 (Fall & Winter, 1967): 10-37, and *Dream Animals: Writings by James Hillman, Paintings by Margot McLean* (San Francisco, CA: Chronicle Books, 1997).
38. C. G. Jung, "Man and his Environment," interview with Hans Carol, 1950/1963, in *C. G. Jung Speaking: Interviews and Encounters*, ed. William McGuire and R. F. C. Hull (Princeton, NJ: Princeton University Press, 1977), p. 202. In this case the translation is mine, from the German text in *C. G. Jung im Gespräch: Interviews, Reden, Begegnungen* (Einsiedeln, Switzerland: Daimon Verlag, 1986), p. 58.

39. Luigi Zoja, *Ethics and Analysis: Philosophical Perspectives and the Application in Therapy*, The Fay Lectures for 2006 (College Station, TX: Texas A&M University Press, 2007).
40. *Pan and the Nightmare: Two Essays by Wilhelm Heinrich Roscher and James Hillman* (Zurich: Spring Publications, 1972).
41. James Hillman, *A Terrible Love of War* (New York: Penguin Books, 2004), p. 197. While both Hillman and Zoja make use of René Girard's writings on violence and the sacred, particularly on the notion of the scapegoat, Hillman's sidestepping of ethology means that only Zoja makes "the other" part of a nightmare scenario, extrapolating that construction backwards from ethology, along the curve of Jung's thinking, to take up the anthropological findings used by Jung on the herd psychology of archaic identity. That anthropology, and the ethological supplement given to it now, supply to Jung's view what the primal scene of parricide gave to Freud's, but free of the Lamarckian overtones in the latter. While both Hillman and Zoja forcefully underline propaganda inflations of a scapegoated enemy, Hillman's projected figure of the enemy lacks a certain dimensionality, whereas Zoja, glancing over his shoulder to ethology, treats the enemy more deeply as the feared object of primal separation in ego formation.
42. Eric Voegelin, *The World of the Polis*, vol. 2 of *Order and History* (Baton Rouge, LA: Louisiana State University Press, 1957), p. 251.
43. See Elizabeth Craik, "Tragedy as Treatment: Medical Analogies in Aristotle's Poetics," in *Dionysalexandros: Essays on Aeschylus and His Fellow Tragedians in Honour of Alexander F. Garvie*, ed. Douglas Cairns and Vayos Liapis (Swansea, UK: Classical Press of Wales, 2006), pp. 283-299.
44. Zoja, *Cultivating the Soul*, in particular Chapter 14, "The *Agamemnon* and the Contemporary Presence of Tragedy"; Chapter 17, "Analysis and Tragedy"; and Chapter 8, "Individuation and Paideia."
45. Zoja, *Ethics and Analysis*, pp. 39-41 *et passim.*
46. Zoja, *Cultivating the Soul*, p. 173.
47. Donald Kalsched, *The Inner World of Trauma: Archetypal Defenses of the Personal Spirit* (London: Routledge, 1996).
48. C. G. Jung, *Letters*, vol. 1: 1906-1950, ed. Gerhard Adler and Aniela Jaffé, trans. R. F. C. Hull, Bollingen Series XCV:1 (Princeton, NJ: Princeton University Press, 1973), p. 364.
49. Terry Eagleton, *Sweet Violence: The Idea of the Tragic* (Malden, MA: Blackwell, 2003). Walter Benjamin, "Critique of Violence" (1921), in *Walter Benjamin: Selected Writings, vol. 1, 1913-1926*, ed. Marcus Bullock and Michael Jennings (Cambridge, MA: Belknap/Harvard University Press, 1996).
50. C. G. Jung, *Letters*, vol. 2: 1951-1961 (Princeton, NJ: Princeton University Press, 1975) p. 436 (to Morton Kelsey, 3 May 1958, original in English).

Index

A

D

F

P

T

SPRING JOURNAL BOOKS

The book publishing imprint of *Spring Journal*, the oldest Jungian psychology journal in the world

HOW TO ORDER:

Mail: Spring Journal Books, 627 Ursulines Street # 7, New Orleans, Louisiana 70116, USA
Tel.: (504) 524-5117; **Website:** www.springjournalandbooks.com

STUDIES IN ARCHETYPAL PSYCHOLOGY SERIES
Series Editor: Greg Mogenson

Collected English Papers, Wolfgang Giegerich
 Vol. 1: *The Neurosis of Psychology: Primary Papers Towards a Critical Psychology*, ISBN 978-1-882670-42-0, 284 pp., $20.00
 Vol. 2: *Technology and the Soul: From the Nuclear Bomb to the World Wide Web*, ISBN 978-1-882670-43-4, 356 pp., $25.00
 Vol. 3: *Soul-Violence* ISBN 978-1-882670-44-4, 476 pp., $ 32.95.
 Vol. 4: *The Soul Always Thinks* ISBN 978-1-882670-45-1.

Dialectics & Analytical Psychology: The El Capitan Canyon Seminar, Wolfgang Giegerich, David L. Miller, and Greg Mogenson, ISBN 978-1-882670-92-5, 136 pp., $20.00

Northern Gnosis: Thor, Baldr, and the Volsungs in the Thought of Freud and Jung, Greg Mogenson, ISBN 978-1-882670-90-1, 140 pp., $20.00

Raids on the Unthinkable: Freudian and Jungian Psychoanalyses, Paul Kugler, ISBN 978-1-882670-91-8, 160 pp., $20.00

The Essentials of Style: A Handbook for Seeing and Being Seen, Benjamin Sells, ISBN 978-1-882670-68-0, 165 pp., $21.95

The Wounded Researcher: A Depth Psychological Approach to Research, Robert Romanyshyn, ISBN 978-1-882670-47-5, 360 pp., $24.95

The Sunken Quest, the Wasted Fisher, the Pregnant Fish: Postmodern Reflections on Depth Psychology, Ronald Schenk, ISBN 978-1-882670-48-2, 166 pp., $20.00

Fire in the Stone: The Alchemy of Desire, Stanton Marlan, ed., ISBN 978-1-882670-49-3, 176 pp., $22.95

After Prophecy: Imagination, Incarnation, and the Unity of the Prophetic Tradition, Tom Cheetham, ISBN 978-1-882670-81-9, 183 pp., $22.95

Archetypal Psychologies: Reflections in Honor of James Hillman, Stanton Marlan, ed., ISBN 978-1-882670-54-3, 526 pp. $32.95

Honoring David L. Miller

Disturbances in the Field: Essays in Honor of David L. Miller, Christine Downing, ed., ISBN 978-1-882670-37-6, 318 pp., $23.95

The David L. Miller Trilogy

Three Faces of God: Traces of the Trinity in Literature and Life, David L. Miller, ISBN 978-1-882670-94-9, 197 pp., $20.00

Christs: Meditations on Archetypal Images in Christian Theology, David L. Miller, ISBN 978-1-882670-93-2, 249 pp., $20.00

Hells and Holy Ghosts: A Theopoetics of Christian Belief, David L. Miller, ISBN 978-1-882670-97-0, 238 pp., $20.00

The Electra Series

Electra: Tracing a Feminine Myth through the Western Imagination, Nancy Cater, ISBN 978-1-882670-98-7, 137 pp., $20.00

Fathers' Daughters: Breaking the Ties That Bind, Maureen Murdock, ISBN 978-1-882670-31-4, 258 pp., $20.00

Daughters of Saturn: From Father's Daughter to Creative Woman, Patricia Reis, ISBN 978-1-882670-32-1, 361 pp., $23.95

Women's Mysteries: Twoard a Poetics of Gender, Christine Downing, ISBN 978-1-882670-99-4, 237 pp., $20.00

Gods in Our Midst: Mythological Images of the Masculine—A Woman's View, Christine Downing, ISBN 978-1-882670-28-4, 152 pp., $20.00

Journey through Menopause: A Personal Rite of Passage, Christine Downing, ISBN 978-1-882670-33-8, 172 pp., $20.00

Psyche's Sisters: Reimagining the Meaning of Sisterhood, Christine Downing, ISBN 978-1-882670-74-1, 177 pp., $20.00

Portrait of the Blue Lady: The Character of Melancholy, Lyn Cowan, ISBN 978-1-882670-96-3, 314 pp., $23.95

Jungian Odyssey Series

Volume I

Intimacy: Venturing the Uncertainties of the Heart, Isabelle Meier, Stacy Wirth, and John Hill, eds., ISBN 978-1-882670-84-0, 225 pp., $24.95

More Spring Journal Books

Field, Form, and Fate: Patterns in Mind, Nature, and Psyche, Michael Conforti, ISBN 978-1-882670-40-6, 181 pp., $20.00

The Betrayal of the Soul in Psychotherapy, Robert Stein, ISBN 978-1-882670-16-1, 195 pp., $19.00

Love, Sex, and Marriage: Collected Essays of Robert Stein, Robert Stein, ISBN 978-1-882670-20-8, 382 pp. $19.00

Dark Voices: The Genesis of Roy Hart Theatre, Noah Pikes, ISBN 978-1-882670-19-2, 155 pp., $20.00

The World Turned Inside Out: Henry Corbin and Islamic Mysticism, Tom Cheetham, ISBN 978-1-882670-24-6, 210 pp., $20.00

Teachers of Myth: Interviews on Educational and Psychological Uses of Myth with Adolescents, Maren Tonder Hansen, ISBN 978-1-882670-89-5, 73 pp., $15.95

Following the Reindeer Woman: Path of Peace and Harmony, Linda Schierse Leonard, ISBN 978-1-882670-95-6, 229 pp., $20.00

An Oedipus—The Untold Story: A Ghostly Mythodrama in One Act, Armando Nascimento Rosa, ISBN 978-1-882670-38-3, 103 pp., $20.00

The Dreaming Way: Dreamwork and Art for Remembering and Recovery, Patricia Reis and Susan Snow, ISBN 978-1-882670-46-8, 174 pp. $24.95

Living with Jung: "Enterviews" with Jungian Analysts, Volume 1, Robert and Janis Henderson, ISBN 978-1-882670-35-2, 225 pp., $21.95

Living with Jung: "Enterviews" with Jungian Analysts, Volume 2, Robert and Janis Henderson, ISBN 978-1-882670-72-7, 275 pp., $23.95.

Terraspychology: Re-engaging the Soul of Place, Craig Chalquist, ISBN978-1-882670-65-9, 158 pp., $21.95

Psyche and the Sacred: Spirituality beyond Religion, Lionel Corbet, ISBN978-1-882670-34-5, 350 pp., $23.95

Brothers and Sisters: Discovering the Psychology of Companionship, Lara Newton, ISBN 978-1-882670-70-1, 310 pp., $24.95

Evocations of Absence: Multidisciplinary Perspectives on Void States, Paul W. Ashton, ed., ISBN 978-1-882670-75-8, 214 pp., $22.95

Clio's Circle: Entering The Imaginal World of Historians, Ruth Meyer, ISBN 978-1-882670-70-3, 325 pp., $23.95

Sexuality and the Religious Imagination, Bradley A. TePaske, ISBN: 978-1-882670-51-2, 299 pp., $ 27.95

Mortally Wounded: Stories of Soul Pain, Death, and Healing, Michael Kearney, ISBN 978-1-882670-79-6, 157 pp., $19.95

Dream Tending, Stephen Aizenstat, ISBN 978-0-882670-55-0, 287 pp., $38.00 (hardcover).

The War of the Gods in Addiction: C. G. Jung, Alcoholics Anonymous, and Archetypal Evil, David E. Schoen, ISBN 978-1-882670-57-4, 172 pp., $23.95

C. G. Jung and the Sioux Traditions: Dreams, Visions, Nature, and the Primitive, Vine Deloria, Jr., edited by Philip J. Deloria and Jerome S. Bernstein, ISBN 978-1-882670-61-1, 292 pp., $25.95

Reimagining Education: Essays on Reviving the Soul of Learning, Dennis Patrick Slattery and Jennifer Leigh Selig, eds., ISBN 978-1-882670-63-5, 212 pp., $25.95

Imagination & Medicine: The Future of Healing in an Age of Neuroscience, Stephen Aizenstat and Robert Bosnak, eds., ISBN 978-1-882670-62-8, 212pp., $24.95

A Place of Healing: Working with Nature & Soul at the End of Life, Michael Kearney, M.D., ISBN 978-1-882670-58-1, 292 pp., $23.95.

Woman Changing Woman: Restoring the Mother-Daughter Relationship, Virginia Beane Rutter, ISBN 978-1-882670-83-3, 303 pp., $25.95